THE SUBTLE ART OF
NOT GIVING A FUCK

The Subtle Art of Not Giving a Fuck

*A Counterintuitive Approach
to Living a Good Life*

MARK MANSON

HARPER

An Imprint of HarperCollins*Publishers*

HarperOne

HarperCollins books may be purchased for educational, business, or sales promotional use. For information, please email the Special Markets Department at SPsales@harpercollins.com.

First HarperOne hardcover published 2016.

FIRST EDITION

Designed by Joan Olson

Library of Congress Cataloging-in-Publication Data has been applied for.

ISBN 978–0–06–283750–9

22   CPI 16

Printed and bound by CPI Group (UK) Ltd, Croydon CR0 4YY

Contents

THE SUBTLE ART OF NOT GIVING A FUCK

Don't Try

C harles Bukowski was an alcoholic, a womanizer, a chronic gambler, a lout, a cheapskate, a deadbeat, and on his worst days, a poet. He's probably the last person on earth you would ever look to for life advice or expect to see in any sort of self-help book.

Which is why he's the perfect place to start.

Bukowski wanted to be a writer. But for decades his work was rejected by almost every magazine, newspaper, journal, agent, and publisher he submitted to. His work was horrible, they said. Crude. Disgusting. Depraved. And as the stacks of rejection slips piled up, the weight of his failures pushed him deep into an alcohol-fueled depression that would follow him for most of his life.

Bukowski had a day job as a letter-filer at a post office. He got paid shit money and spent most of it on booze. He gambled away the rest at the racetrack. At night, he would drink alone and sometimes hammer out poetry on his beat-up old typewriter. Often, he'd wake up on the floor, having passed out the night before.

Thirty years went by like this, most of it a meaningless blur of alcohol, drugs, gambling, and prostitutes. Then, when Bukowski was fifty, after a lifetime of failure and self-loathing, an editor at a small independent publishing house took a strange interest in him. The editor couldn't offer Bukowski much money or much promise of sales. But he had a weird affection for the drunk loser, so he decided to take a chance on him. It was the first real shot Bukowski had ever gotten, and, he realized, probably the only one he would ever get. Bukowski wrote back to the editor: "I have one of two choices—stay in the post office and go crazy . . . or stay out here and play at writer and starve. I have decided to starve."

Upon signing the contract, Bukowski wrote his first novel in three weeks. It was called simply *Post Office*. In the dedication, he wrote, "Dedicated to nobody."

Bukowski would make it as a novelist and poet. He would go on and publish six novels and hundreds of poems, selling over two million copies of his books. His popularity defied everyone's expectations, particularly his own.

Stories like Bukowski's are the bread and butter of our cultural narrative. Bukowski's life embodies the American Dream: a man fights for what he wants, never gives up, and eventually achieves his wildest dreams. It's practically a movie waiting to happen. We all look at stories like Bukowski's and say, "See? He never gave up. He never stopped trying. He always believed in himself. He persisted against all the odds and made something of himself!"

It is then strange that on Bukowski's tombstone, the epitaph reads: "Don't try."

See, despite the book sales and the fame, Bukowski was a loser. He knew it. And his success stemmed not from some determination to be a winner, but from the fact that he *knew* he was a loser, accepted it, and then wrote honestly about it. He never tried to be anything other than what he was. The genius in Bukowski's work was not in overcoming unbelievable odds or developing himself into a shining literary light. It was the opposite. It was his simple ability to be completely, unflinchingly honest with himself—especially the worst parts of himself—and to share his failings without hesitation or doubt.

This is the real story of Bukowski's success: his comfort with himself as a failure. Bukowski didn't give a fuck about success. Even after his fame, he still showed up to poetry readings hammered and verbally abused people in his audience. He still exposed himself in public and tried to sleep with every woman he could find. Fame and success didn't make him a better person. Nor was it by becoming a better person that he became famous and successful.

Self-improvement and success often occur together. But that doesn't necessarily mean they're the same thing.

Our culture today is obsessively focused on unrealistically positive expectations: Be happier. Be healthier. Be the best, better than the rest. Be smarter, faster, richer, sexier, more popular, more productive, more envied, and more admired. Be perfect and amazing and crap out twelve-karat-gold nuggets before breakfast each morning while kissing your selfie-ready spouse and two and a half kids goodbye. Then fly your helicopter to your wonderfully fulfilling job, where you spend your days doing incredibly meaningful work that's likely to save the planet one day.

But when you stop and really think about it, conventional life advice—all the positive and happy self-help stuff we hear all the time—is actually fixating on what you *lack*. It lasers in on *what you perceive your personal shortcomings and failures to already be*, and then emphasizes them for you. You learn about the best ways to make money *because* you feel you don't have enough money already. You stand in front of the mirror and repeat affirmations saying that you're beautiful *because* you feel as though you're not beautiful already. You follow dating and relationship advice *because* you feel that you're unlovable already. You try goofy visualization exercises about being more successful *because* you feel as though you aren't successful enough already.

Ironically, this fixation on the positive—on what's better, what's superior—only serves to remind us over and over again of what we are not, of what we lack, of what we should have been but failed to be. After all, no truly happy person feels the need to stand in front of a mirror and recite that she's happy. She just *is*.

There's a saying in Texas: "The smallest dog barks the loudest." A confident man doesn't feel a need to prove that he's confident. A rich woman doesn't feel a need to convince anybody that she's rich. Either you are or you are not. And if you're dreaming of something all the time, then you're reinforcing the same unconscious reality over and over: that you are *not that.*

Everyone and their TV commercial wants you to believe that the key to a good life is a nicer job, or a more rugged car, or a prettier girlfriend, or a hot tub with an inflatable pool for the kids. The world is constantly telling you that the path to a better life is more, more, more—buy more, own more, make more, fuck more, *be* more. You are constantly bombarded with messages to give a fuck about everything, all the time. Give a fuck about a new TV. Give a fuck about having a better vacation than your coworkers. Give a fuck about buying that new lawn ornament. Give a fuck about having the right kind of selfie stick.

Why? My guess: because giving a fuck about more stuff is good for business.

And while there's nothing wrong with good business, the problem is that giving too many fucks is bad for your mental health. It causes you to become overly attached to the superficial and fake, to dedicate your life to chasing a mirage of happiness and satisfaction. The key to a good life is not giving a fuck about more; it's giving a fuck about less, giving a fuck about only what is true and immediate and important.

The Feedback Loop from Hell

There's an insidious quirk to your brain that, if you let it, can drive you absolutely batty. Tell me if this sounds familiar to you:

You get anxious about confronting somebody in your life. That anxiety cripples you and you start wondering why you're so anxious. Now you're becoming *anxious about being anxious.* Oh no! Doubly anxious! Now you're anxious about your anxiety, which is causing *more* anxiety. Quick, where's the whiskey?

Or let's say you have an anger problem. You get pissed off at the stupidest, most inane stuff, and you have no idea why. And the fact that you get pissed off so easily starts to piss you off even more. And then, in your petty rage, you realize that being angry all the time makes you a shallow and mean person, and you hate this; you hate it so much that you get angry at yourself. Now look at you: you're angry at yourself getting angry about being angry. Fuck you, wall. Here, have a fist.

Or you're so worried about doing the right thing all the time that you become worried about how much you're worrying. Or you feel so guilty for every mistake you make that you begin to feel guilty about how guilty you're feeling. Or you get sad and alone so often that it makes you feel even more sad and alone just thinking about it.

Welcome to the Feedback Loop from Hell. Chances are you've engaged in it more than a few times. Maybe you're engaging in it right now: "God, I do the Feedback Loop all the time—I'm such a loser for doing it. I should stop. Oh my God, I feel like such a loser for calling myself a loser. I should stop calling myself a loser. Ah, fuck! I'm doing it again! See? I'm a loser! Argh!"

Calm down, amigo. Believe it or not, this is part of the

beauty of being human. Very few animals on earth have the ability to think cogent thoughts to begin with, but we humans have the luxury of being able to have thoughts *about* our thoughts. So I can think about watching Miley Cyrus videos on YouTube, and then immediately think about what a sicko I am for wanting to watch Miley Cyrus videos on YouTube. Ah, the miracle of consciousness!

Now here's the problem: Our society today, through the wonders of consumer culture and hey-look-my-life-is-cooler-than-yours social media, has bred a whole generation of people who believe that having these negative experiences—anxiety, fear, guilt, etc.—is totally not okay. I mean, if you look at your Facebook feed, everybody there is having a fucking grand old time. Look, eight people got married this week! And some sixteen-year-old on TV got a Ferrari for her birthday. And another kid just made two billion dollars inventing an app that automatically delivers you more toilet paper when you run out.

Meanwhile, you're stuck at home flossing your cat. And you can't help but think your life sucks even more than you thought.

The Feedback Loop from Hell has become a borderline epidemic, making many of us overly stressed, overly neurotic, and overly self-loathing.

Back in Grandpa's day, he would feel like shit and think to himself, "Gee whiz, I sure do feel like a cow turd today. But hey, I guess that's just life. Back to shoveling hay."

But now? Now if you feel like shit for even five minutes, you're bombarded with 350 images of people *totally happy and having amazing fucking lives,* and it's impossible to not feel like there's something wrong with you.

It's this last part that gets us into trouble. We feel bad about feeling bad. We feel guilty for feeling guilty. We get angry about getting angry. We get anxious about feeling anxious. *What is wrong with me?*

This is why not giving a fuck is so key. This is why it's going to save the world. And it's going to save it by accepting that the world is totally fucked and that's all right, because it's always been that way, and always will be.

By not giving a fuck that you feel bad, you short-circuit the Feedback Loop from Hell; you say to yourself, "I feel like shit, but who gives a fuck?" And then, as if sprinkled by magic fuck-giving fairy dust, you stop hating yourself for feeling so bad.

George Orwell said that to see what's in front of one's nose requires a constant struggle. Well, the solution to our stress and anxiety is right there in front of our noses, and we're too busy watching porn and advertisements for ab machines that don't work, wondering why we're not banging a hot blonde with a rocking six-pack, to notice.

We joke online about "first-world problems," but we really have become victims of our own success. Stress-related health issues, anxiety disorders, and cases of depression have skyrocketed over the past thirty years, despite the fact that everyone has a flat-screen TV and can have their groceries delivered. Our crisis is no longer material; it's existential, it's spiritual. We have so much fucking stuff and so many opportunities that we don't even know what to give a fuck about anymore.

Because there's an infinite amount of things we can now see or know, there are also an infinite number of ways we can discover that we don't measure up, that we're not good enough, that things aren't as great as they could be. And this rips us apart inside.

Because here's the thing that's wrong with all of the "How to Be Happy" shit that's been shared eight million times on Facebook in the past few years—here's what nobody realizes about all of this crap:

> **The desire for more positive experience is itself a negative experience. And, paradoxically, the acceptance of one's negative experience is itself a positive experience.**

This is a total mind-fuck. So I'll give you a minute to unpretzel your brain and maybe read that again: *Wanting positive experience is a negative experience; accepting negative experience is a positive experience.* It's what the philosopher Alan Watts used to refer to as "the backwards law"—the idea that the more you pursue feeling better all the time, the less satisfied you become, as pursuing something only reinforces the fact that you lack it in the first place. The more you desperately want to be rich, the more poor and unworthy you feel, regardless of how much money you actually make. The more you desperately want to be sexy and desired, the uglier you come to see yourself, regardless of your actual physical appearance. The more you desperately want to be happy and loved, the lonelier and more afraid you become, regardless of those who surround you. The more you want to be spiritually enlightened, the more self-centered and shallow you become in trying to get there.

It's like this one time I tripped on acid and it felt like the more I walked toward a house, the farther away the house got from me. And yes, I just used my LSD hallucinations to make a philosophical point about happiness. No fucks given.

As the existential philosopher Albert Camus said (and I'm pretty sure he wasn't on LSD at the time): "You will never be happy if you continue to search for what happiness consists of. You will never live if you are looking for the meaning of life."

Or put more simply:

Don't try.

Now, I know what you're saying: "Mark, this is making my nipples all hard, but what about the Camaro I've been saving up for? What about the beach body I've been starving myself for? After all, I paid a lot of money for that ab machine! What about the big house on the lake I've been dreaming of? If I stop giving a fuck about those things—well, then I'll never achieve *anything*. I don't want that to happen, do I?"

So glad you asked.

Ever notice that sometimes when you care *less* about something, you do better at it? Notice how it's often the person who is the least invested in the success of something that actually ends up achieving it? Notice how sometimes when you stop giving a fuck, everything seems to fall into place?

What's with that?

What's interesting about the backwards law is that it's called "backwards" for a reason: not giving a fuck works in reverse. If pursuing the positive *is* a negative, then pursuing the negative generates the positive. The pain you pursue in the gym results in better all-around health and energy. The failures in business are what lead to a better understanding of what's necessary to be successful. Being open with your insecurities paradoxically makes you more confident and charismatic around others. The pain of honest confrontation is what generates the greatest trust and respect in your relationships. Suffering through your fears and anxieties is what allows you to build courage and perseverance.

Seriously, I could keep going, but you get the point. *Everything worthwhile in life is won through surmounting the associated negative experience.* Any attempt to escape the negative, to avoid it or quash it or silence it, only backfires. The avoidance of suffering *is* a form of suffering. The avoidance of struggle *is* a struggle. The denial of failure *is* a failure. Hiding what is shameful *is* itself a form of shame.

Pain is an inextricable thread in the fabric of life, and to tear it out is not only impossible, but destructive: attempting to tear it out unravels everything else with it. To try to avoid pain is to give too many fucks about pain. In contrast, if you're able to not give a fuck about the pain, you become unstoppable.

In my life, I have given a fuck about many things. I have also *not* given a fuck about many things. And like the road not taken, it was the fucks not given that made all the difference.

Chances are you know somebody in your life who, at one time or another, did not give a fuck and then went on to accomplish amazing feats. Perhaps there was a time in your own life when you simply did not give a fuck and excelled to some extraordinary height. For myself, quitting my day job in finance after only six weeks to start an Internet business ranks pretty high up there in my own "didn't give a fuck" hall of fame. Same with deciding to sell most of my possessions and move to South America. Fucks given? None. Just went and did it.

These moments of non-fuckery are the moments that most define our lives. The major switch in careers; the spontaneous choice to drop out of college and join a rock band; the decision to finally dump that deadbeat boyfriend whom you caught wearing your pantyhose a few too many times.

To not give a fuck is to stare down life's most terrifying and difficult challenges and still take action.

While not giving a fuck may seem simple on the surface, it's a whole new bag of burritos under the hood. I don't even know what that sentence means, but I don't give a fuck. A bag of burritos sounds awesome, so let's just go with it.

Most of us struggle throughout our lives by giving too many fucks in situations where fucks do not deserve to be given. We give too many fucks about the rude gas station attendant who gave us our change in nickels. We give too many fucks when a show we liked was canceled on TV. We give too many fucks when our coworkers don't bother asking us about our awesome weekend.

Meanwhile, our credit cards are maxed out, our dog hates us, and Junior is snorting meth in the bathroom, yet we're getting pissed off about nickels and *Everybody Loves Raymond.*

Look, this is how it works. You're going to die one day. I know that's kind of obvious, but I just wanted to remind you in case you'd forgotten. You and everyone you know are going to be dead soon. And in the short amount of time between here and there, you have a limited amount of fucks to give. Very few, in fact. And if you go around giving a fuck about everything and everyone without conscious thought or choice—well, then you're going to get fucked.

There is a subtle art to not giving a fuck. And though the concept may sound ridiculous and I may sound like an asshole, what I'm talking about here is essentially learning how to focus and prioritize your thoughts effectively—how to pick and choose what matters to you and what does not matter to you based on finely honed personal values. This is incredibly difficult. It takes a lifetime of practice and discipline to achieve. And you will regularly fail. But it is perhaps the most worthy struggle one can undertake in one's life. It is perhaps the *only* struggle in one's life.

Because when you give too many fucks—when you give a fuck about everyone and everything—you will feel that you're perpetually entitled to be comfortable and happy at all times, that everything is supposed to be just exactly the fucking way *you* want it to be. This is a sickness. And it will eat you alive. You will see every adversity as an injustice, every challenge as a failure, every inconvenience as a personal slight, every disagreement as a betrayal. You will be confined to your own petty, skull-sized hell, burning with entitlement and bluster, running circles around your very own personal Feedback Loop from Hell, in constant motion yet arriving nowhere.

The Subtle Art of Not Giving a Fuck

When most people envision giving no fucks whatsoever, they imagine a kind of serene indifference to everything, a calm that weathers all storms. They imagine and aspire to be a person who is shaken by nothing and caves in to no one.

There's a name for a person who finds no emotion or meaning in anything: a psychopath. Why you would want to emulate a psychopath, I have no fucking clue.

So what *does* not giving a fuck mean? Let's look at three "subtleties" that should help clarify the matter.

> *Subtlety #1: Not giving a fuck does not mean being indifferent; it means being comfortable with being different.*

Let's be clear. There's absolutely nothing admirable or confident about indifference. People who are indifferent are lame and scared. They're couch potatoes and Internet trolls. In fact, indifferent people often attempt to be indifferent because in reality they give way too many fucks. They give a fuck about what everyone thinks of their hair, so they never bother washing or combing it. They give a fuck about what everyone thinks of their ideas, so they hide behind sarcasm and self-righteous snark. They're afraid to let anyone get close to them, so they imagine themselves as some special, unique snowflake who has problems that nobody else would ever understand.

Indifferent people are afraid of the world and the repercussions of their own choices. That's why they don't make any meaningful choices. They hide in a gray, emotionless pit of their own making, self-absorbed and self-pitying, perpetually distracting themselves from this unfortunate thing demanding their time and energy called life.

Because here's a sneaky truth about life. There's no such thing as not giving a fuck. *You must give a fuck about something.* It's part of our biology to always care about something and therefore to always give a fuck.

The question, then, is, *What* do we give a fuck about? What are we *choosing* to give a fuck about? And how can we not give a fuck about what ultimately does not matter?

My mother was recently screwed out of a large chunk of money by a close friend of hers. Had I been indifferent, I would have shrugged my shoulders, sipped my mocha, and downloaded another season of *The Wire*. Sorry, Mom.

But instead, I was indignant. I was pissed off. I said, "No, screw that, Mom. We're going to lawyer the fuck up and go after this asshole. Why? Because I don't give a fuck. I will ruin this guy's life if I have to."

This illustrates the first subtlety of not giving a fuck. When we say, "Damn, watch out, Mark Manson just don't give a fuck," we don't mean that Mark Manson doesn't care about *anything;* on the contrary, we mean that Mark Manson doesn't care about adversity in the face of his goals, he doesn't care about pissing some people off to do what he feels is right or important or noble. We mean that Mark Manson is the type of guy who would write about himself in third person just because he thought it was the right thing to do. He just doesn't give a fuck.

This is what is so admirable. No, not me, dumbass—the overcoming adversity stuff, the willingness to be different, an outcast, a pariah, all for the sake of one's own values. The willingness to stare failure in the face and shove your middle finger back at it. The people who don't give a fuck about adversity or failure or embarrassing themselves or shitting the bed a few times. The people who just laugh and then do what they believe in anyway. Because they know it's right. They know it's more important than they are, more important than their own feelings and their own pride and their own ego. They say, "Fuck it," not to everything in life, but rather to everything *unimportant* in life. They reserve their fucks for what truly matters. Friends. Family. Purpose. Burritos. And an occasional lawsuit or two. And because of that, because they reserve their fucks for only the big things that matter, people give a fuck about them in return.

Because here's another sneaky little truth about life. You can't be an important and life-changing presence for some people without also being a joke and an embarrassment to others. You just can't. Because there's no such thing as a lack of adversity. It doesn't exist. The old saying goes that no matter where you go, there you are. Well, the same is true for adversity and failure. No matter where you go, there's a five-hundred-pound load of shit waiting for you. And that's perfectly fine. The point isn't to get away from the shit. The point is to find the shit you enjoy dealing with.

Subtlety #2: To not give a fuck about adversity, you must first give a fuck about something more important than adversity.

Imagine you're at a grocery store, and you watch an elderly lady scream at the cashier, berating him for not accepting her thirty-cent coupon. Why does this lady give a fuck? It's just thirty cents.

I'll tell you why: That lady probably doesn't have anything better to do with her days than to sit at home cutting out coupons. She's old and lonely. Her kids are dickheads and never visit. She hasn't had sex in over thirty years. She can't fart without extreme lower-back pain. Her pension is on its last legs, and she's probably going to die in a diaper thinking she's in Candy Land.

So she snips coupons. That's all she's got. It's her and her damn coupons. It's all she can give a fuck about because there *is* nothing else to give a fuck about. And so when that pimply-faced seventeen-year-old cashier refuses to accept one of them, when he defends his cash register's purity the way knights used to defend maidens' virginity, you can bet Granny is going to erupt. Eighty years of fucks will rain down all at once, like a fiery hailstorm of "Back in my day" and "People used to show more respect" stories.

The problem with people who hand out fucks like ice cream at a goddamn summer camp is that they don't have anything more fuck-worthy to dedicate their fucks to.

If you find yourself consistently giving too many fucks about trivial shit that bothers you—your ex-boyfriend's new Facebook picture, how quickly the batteries die in the TV remote, missing out on yet another two-for-one sale on hand sanitizer—chances are you don't have much going on in your life to give a legitimate fuck about. And that's your real problem. Not the hand sanitizer. Not the TV remote.

I once heard an artist say that when a person has no problems, the mind automatically finds a way to invent some. I think what most people—especially educated, pampered middle-class white people—consider "life problems" are really just side effects of not having anything more important to worry about.

It then follows that finding something important and meaningful in your life is perhaps the most productive use of your time and energy. Because if you don't find that meaningful something, your fucks will be given to meaningless and frivolous causes.

Subtlety #3: Whether you realize it or not, you are always choosing what to give a fuck about.

People aren't just born not giving a fuck. In fact, we're born giving way too many fucks. Ever watch a kid cry his eyes out because his hat is the wrong shade of blue? Exactly. Fuck that kid.

When we're young, everything is new and exciting, and everything seems to matter so much. Therefore, we give tons of fucks. We give a fuck about everything and everyone— about what people are saying about us, about whether that cute boy/girl called us back or not, about whether our socks match or not, or what color our birthday balloon is.

As we get older, with the benefit of experience (and having seen so much time slip by), we begin to notice that most of these sorts of things have little lasting impact on our lives. Those people whose opinions we cared about so much before are no longer present in our lives. Rejections that were painful in the moment have actually worked out for the best. We realize how little attention people pay to the superficial details about us, and we choose not to obsess so much over them.

Essentially, we become more selective about the fucks we're willing to give. This is something called maturity. It's nice; you should try it sometime. Maturity is what happens when one learns to only give a fuck about what's truly fuck-worthy. As Bunk Moreland said to his partner Detective McNulty in *The Wire* (which, fuck you, I still downloaded): "That's what you get for giving a fuck when it wasn't your turn to give a fuck."

Then, as we grow older and enter middle age, something else begins to change. Our energy level drops. Our identity solidifies. We know who we are and we accept ourselves, including some of the parts we aren't thrilled about.

And, in a strange way, this is liberating. We no longer need to give a fuck about everything. Life is just what it is. We accept it, warts and all. We realize that we're never going to cure cancer or go to the moon or feel Jennifer Aniston's tits. And that's okay. Life goes on. We now reserve our ever-dwindling fucks for the most truly fuck-worthy parts of our lives: our families, our best friends, our golf swing. And, to our astonishment, *this is enough*. This simplification actually makes us really fucking happy on a consistent basis. And we start to think, Maybe that crazy alcoholic Bukowski was onto something. *Don't try.*

So Mark, What the Fuck Is the Point of This Book Anyway?

This book will help you think a little bit more clearly about what you're choosing to find important in life and what you're choosing to find unimportant.

I believe that today we're facing a psychological epidemic, one in which people no longer realize it's okay for things to suck sometimes. I know that sounds intellectually lazy on the surface, but I promise you, it's a life/death sort of issue.

Because when we believe that it's not okay for things to suck sometimes, then we unconsciously start blaming ourselves. We start to feel as though something is inherently wrong with us, which drives us to all sorts of overcompensation, like buying forty pairs of shoes or downing Xanax with a vodka chaser on a Tuesday night or shooting up a school bus full of kids.

This belief that it's not okay to be inadequate sometimes is the source of the growing Feedback Loop from Hell that is coming to dominate our culture.

The idea of not giving a fuck is a simple way of reorienting our expectations for life and choosing what is important and what is not. Developing this ability leads to something I like to think of as a kind of "practical enlightenment."

No, not that airy-fairy, eternal bliss, end-of-all-suffering, bullshitty kind of enlightenment. On the contrary, I see practical enlightenment as becoming comfortable with the idea that some suffering is always inevitable—that no matter what you do, life is comprised of failures, loss, regrets, and even death. Because once you become comfortable with all the shit that life throws at you (and it will throw a lot of shit, trust me), you become invincible in a sort of low-level spiritual way. After all, the only way to overcome pain is to first learn how to bear it.

This book doesn't give a fuck about alleviating your problems or your pain. And that is precisely why you will know it's being honest. This book is not some guide to greatness—it couldn't be, because greatness is merely an illusion in our minds, a made-up destination that we obligate ourselves to pursue, our own psychological Atlantis.

Instead, this book will turn your pain into a tool, your trauma into power, and your problems into slightly better problems. That is real progress. Think of it as a guide to suffering and how to do it better, more meaningfully, with more compassion and more humility. It's a book about moving lightly despite your heavy burdens, resting easier with your greatest fears, laughing at your tears as you cry them.

This book will not teach you how to gain or achieve, but rather how to lose and let go. It will teach you to take inventory of your life and scrub out all but the most important items. It will teach you to close your eyes and trust that you can fall backwards and still be okay. It will teach you to give fewer fucks. It will teach you to not try.

CHAPTER

2

Happiness Is a Problem

About twenty-five hundred years ago, in the Himalayan foothills of present-day Nepal, there lived in a great palace a king who was going to have a son. For this son the king had a particularly grand idea: he would make the child's life perfect. The child would never know a moment of suffering—every need, every desire, would be accounted for at all times.

The king built high walls around the palace that prevented the prince from knowing the outside world. He spoiled the child, lavishing him with food and gifts, surrounding him with servants who catered to his every whim. And just as planned, the child grew up ignorant of the routine cruelties of human existence.

All of the prince's childhood went on like this. But despite the endless luxury and opulence, the prince became kind of a pissed-off young man. Soon, every experience felt empty and valueless. The problem was that no matter what his father gave him, it never seemed enough, never *meant* anything.

So late one night, the prince snuck out of the palace to see what was beyond its walls. He had a servant drive him through the local village, and what he saw horrified him.

For the first time in his life, the prince saw human suffering. He saw sick people, old people, homeless people, people in pain, even people dying.

The prince returned to the palace and found himself in a sort of existential crisis. Not knowing how to process what he'd seen, he got all emo about everything and complained a lot. And, as is so typical of young men, the prince ended up blaming his father for the very things his father had tried to do for him. It was the riches, the prince thought, that had made him so miserable, that had made life seem so meaningless. He decided to run away.

But the prince was more like his father than he knew. He had grand ideas too. He wouldn't just run away; he would give up his royalty, his family, and all of his possessions and live in the streets, sleeping in dirt like an animal. There he would starve himself, torture himself, and beg for scraps of food from strangers for the rest of his life.

The next night, the prince snuck out of the palace again, this time never to return. For years he lived as a bum, a discarded and forgotten remnant of society, the dog shit caked to the bottom of the social totem pole. And as planned, the prince suffered greatly. He suffered through disease, hunger, pain, loneliness, and decay. He confronted the brink of death itself, often limited to eating a single nut each day.

A few years went by. Then a few more. And then . . . nothing happened. The prince began to notice that this life of suffering wasn't all that it was cracked up to be. It wasn't bringing him the insight he had desired. It wasn't revealing any deeper mystery of the world or its ultimate purpose.

In fact, the prince came to know what the rest of us have always kind of known: that suffering totally sucks. And it's not necessarily that meaningful either. As with being rich, there is no value in suffering when it's done without purpose. And soon the prince came to the conclusion that his grand idea, like his father's, was in fact a fucking terrible idea and he should probably go do something else instead.

Totally confused, the prince cleaned himself up and went and found a big tree near a river. He decided that he would sit under that tree and not get up until he came up with another grand idea.

As the legend goes, the confused prince sat under that tree for forty-nine days. We won't delve into the biological viability of sitting in the same spot for forty-nine days, but let's just say that in that time the prince came to a number of profound realizations.

One of those realizations was this: that life itself is a form of suffering. The rich suffer because of their riches. The poor suffer because of their poverty. People without a family suffer because they have no family. People with a family suffer because of their family. People who pursue worldly pleasures suffer because of their worldly pleasures.

People who abstain from worldly pleasures suffer because of their abstention.

This isn't to say that all suffering is equal. Some suffering is certainly more painful than other suffering. But we all must suffer nonetheless.

Years later, the prince would build his own philosophy and share it with the world, and this would be its first and central tenet: that pain and loss are inevitable and we should let go of trying to resist them. The prince would later become known as the Buddha. And in case you haven't heard of him, he was kind of a big deal.

There is a premise that underlies a lot of our assumptions and beliefs. The premise is that happiness is algorithmic, that it can be worked for and earned and achieved as if it were getting accepted to law school or building a really complicated Lego set. If I achieve X, then I can be happy. If I look like Y, then I can be happy. If I can be with a person like Z, then I can be happy.

This premise, though, *is the problem.* Happiness is not a solvable equation. Dissatisfaction and unease are inherent parts of human nature and, as we'll see, necessary components to creating consistent happiness. The Buddha argued this from a theological and philosophical perspective. I will make the same argument in this chapter, but I will make it from a biological perspective, and with pandas.

The Misadventures of Disappointment Panda

If I could invent a superhero, I would invent one called Disappointment Panda. He'd wear a cheesy eye mask and a shirt (with a giant capital T on it) that was way too small for his big panda belly, and his superpower would be to tell people harsh truths about themselves that they needed to hear but didn't want to accept.

He would go door-to-door like a Bible salesman and ring doorbells and say things like, "Sure, making a lot of money makes you feel good, but it won't make your kids love you," or "If you have to ask yourself if you trust your wife, then you probably don't," or "What you consider 'friendship' is really just your constant attempts to impress people." Then he'd tell the homeowner to have a nice day and saunter on down to the next house.

It would be awesome. And sick. And sad. And uplifting. And necessary. After all, the greatest truths in life are usually the most unpleasant to hear.

Disappointment Panda would be the hero that none of us would want but all of us would need. He'd be the proverbial vegetables to our mental diet of junk food. He'd make our lives better despite making us feel worse. He'd make us stronger by tearing us down, brighten our future by showing us the darkness. Listening to him would be like watching a movie where the hero dies in the end: you love it even more despite making you feel horrible, because it feels real.

So while we're here, allow me to put on my Disappointment Panda mask and drop another unpleasant truth on you:

We suffer for the simple reason that suffering is biologically useful. It is nature's preferred agent for inspiring change. We have evolved to always live with a certain degree of dissatisfaction and insecurity, because it's the mildly dissatisfied and insecure creature that's going to do the most work to innovate and survive. We are wired to become dissatisfied with whatever we have and satisfied by only what we do not have. This constant dissatisfaction has kept our species fighting and striving, building and conquering. So no—our own pain and misery aren't a bug of human evolution; they're a feature.

Pain, in all of its forms, is our body's most effective means of spurring action. Take something as simple as stubbing your toe. If you're like me, when you stub your toe you scream enough four-letter words to make Pope Francis cry. You also probably blame some poor inanimate object for your suffering. "Stupid table," you say. Or maybe you even go so far as to question your entire interior design philosophy based on your throbbing foot: "What kind of idiot puts a table there anyway? Seriously?"

But I digress. That horrible stubbed-toe-induced pain, the one you and I and the pope hate so much, exists for an important reason. Physical pain is a product of our nervous system, a feedback mechanism to give us a sense of our own physical proportions—where we can and cannot move and what we can and cannot touch. When we exceed those limits, our nervous system duly punishes us to make sure that we pay attention and never do it again.

And this pain, as much as we hate it, *is* useful. Pain is what teaches us what to pay attention to when we're young or careless. It helps show us what's good for us versus what's bad for us. It helps us understand and adhere to our own limitations. It teaches us to not fuck around near hot stoves or stick metal objects into electrical sockets. Therefore, it's not always beneficial to avoid pain and seek pleasure, since pain can, at times, be life-or-death important to our well-being.

But pain is not merely physical. As anyone who has had to sit through the first *Star Wars* prequel can tell you, we humans are capable of experiencing acute psychological pain as well. In fact, research has found that our brains don't register much difference between physical pain and psychological pain. So when I tell you that my first girl-friend cheating on me and leaving me felt like having an ice pick slowly inserted into the center of my heart, that's because, well, it hurt so much I might as well have had an ice pick slowly inserted into the center of my heart.

Like physical pain, our psychological pain is an indica-tion of something out of equilibrium, some limitation that has been exceeded. And like our physical pain, our psycho-logical pain is not necessarily always bad or even undesir-able. In some cases, experiencing emotional or psychological pain can be healthy or necessary. Just like stubbing our toe teaches us to walk into fewer tables, the emotional pain of rejection or failure teaches us how to avoid making the same mistakes in the future.

And this is what's so dangerous about a society that cod-dles itself more and more from the inevitable discomforts of life: we lose the benefits of experiencing healthy doses of pain, a loss that disconnects us from the reality of the world around us.

You may salivate at the thought of a problem-free life full of everlasting happiness and eternal compassion, but back here on earth the problems never cease. Seriously, problems don't end. Disappointment Panda just dropped by. We had margaritas, and he told me all about it: problems never fucking go away, he said—they just improve. Warren Buffett's got money problems; the drunk hobo down at Kwik-E Mart's got money problems. Buffett's just got *better* money problems than the hobo. All of life is like this.

"Life is essentially an endless series of problems, Mark," the panda told me. He sipped his drink and adjusted the little pink umbrella. "The solution to one problem is merely the creation of the next one."

A moment passed, and then I wondered where the fuck the talking panda came from. And while we're at it, who made these margaritas?

"Don't hope for a life without problems," the panda said. "There's no such thing. Instead, hope for a life full of good problems."

And with that, he set his glass down, adjusted his sombrero, and sauntered off into the sunset.

Happiness Comes from Solving Problems

Problems are a constant in life. When you solve your health problem by buying a gym membership, you create new problems, like having to get up early to get to the gym on time, sweating like a meth-head for thirty minutes on an elliptical, and then getting showered and changed for work so you don't stink up the whole office. When you solve your problem of not spending enough time with your partner by designating Wednesday night "date night," you generate new problems, such as figuring out what to do every Wednesday that you both won't hate, making sure you have enough money for nice dinners, rediscovering the chemistry and spark you two feel you've lost, and unraveling the logistics of fucking in a small bathtub filled with too many bubbles.

Problems never stop; they merely get exchanged and/or upgraded.

Happiness comes from solving problems. The keyword here is "solving." If you're avoiding your problems or feel like you don't have any problems, then you're going to make yourself miserable. If you feel like you have problems that you can't solve, you will likewise make yourself miserable. The secret sauce is in the *solving* of the problems, not in not having problems in the first place.

To be happy we need something to solve. Happiness is therefore a form of action; it's an activity, not something that is passively bestowed upon you, not something that you magically discover in a top-ten article on the Huffington Post or from any specific guru or teacher. It doesn't magically appear when you finally make enough money to add on that extra room to the house. You don't find it waiting for you in a place, an idea, a job—or even a book, for that matter.

Happiness is a constant work-in-progress, because solving problems is a constant work-in-progress—the solutions to today's problems will lay the foundation for tomorrow's problems, and so on. True happiness occurs only when you find the problems you enjoy having and enjoy solving.

Sometimes those problems are simple: eating good food, traveling to some new place, winning at the new video game you just bought. Other times those problems are abstract and complicated: fixing your relationship with your mother, finding a career you can feel good about, developing better friendships.

Whatever your problems are, the concept is the same: solve problems; be happy. Unfortunately, for many people, life doesn't feel that simple. That's because they fuck things up in at least one of two ways:

1. *Denial.* Some people deny that their problems exist in the first place. And because they deny reality, they must constantly delude or distract themselves from reality. This may make them feel good in the short term, but it leads to a life of insecurity, neuroticism, and emotional repression.

2. *Victim Mentality.* Some choose to believe that there is nothing they can do to solve their problems, even when they in fact could. Victims seek to blame others for their problems or blame outside circumstances. This may make them feel better in the short term, but it leads to a life of anger, helplessness, and despair.

People deny and blame others for their problems for the simple reason that it's easy and feels good, while solving problems is hard and often feels bad. Forms of blame and denial give us a quick high. They are a way to temporarily escape our problems, and that escape can provide us a quick rush that makes us feel better.

Highs come in many forms. Whether it's a substance like alcohol, the moral righteousness that comes from blaming others, or the thrill of some new risky adventure, highs are shallow and unproductive ways to go about one's life. Much of the self-help world is predicated on peddling highs to people rather than solving legitimate problems. Many self-help gurus teach you new forms of denial and pump you up with exercises that feel good in the short term, while ignoring the underlying issue. Remember, nobody who is actually happy has to stand in front of a mirror and tell himself that he's happy.

Highs also generate addiction. The more you rely on them to feel better about your underlying problems, the more you will seek them out. In this sense, almost anything can become addictive, depending on the motivation behind using it. We all have our chosen methods to numb the pain of our problems, and in moderate doses there is nothing wrong with this. But the longer we avoid and the longer we numb, the more painful it will be when we finally do confront our issues.

Emotions Are Overrated

Emotions evolved for one specific purpose: to help us live and reproduce a little bit better. That's it. They're feedback mechanisms telling us that something is either likely right or likely wrong for us—nothing more, nothing less.

Much as the pain of touching a hot stove teaches you not to touch it again, the sadness of being alone teaches you not to do the things that made you feel so alone again. Emotions are simply biological signals designed to nudge you in the direction of beneficial change.

Look, I don't mean to make light of your midlife crisis or the fact that your drunk dad stole your bike when you were eight years old and you still haven't gotten over it, but when it comes down to it, if you feel crappy it's because your brain is telling you that there's a problem that's unaddressed or unresolved. In other words, negative emotions are a *call to action*. When you feel them, it's because you're supposed to *do something*. Positive emotions, on the other hand, are rewards for taking the proper action. When you feel them, life seems simple and there is nothing else to do but enjoy it. Then, like everything else, the positive emotions go away, because more problems inevitably emerge.

Emotions are part of the equation of our lives, but not the *entire* equation. Just because something feels good doesn't mean it *is* good. Just because something feels bad doesn't mean it *is* bad. Emotions are merely signposts, *suggestions* that our neurobiology gives us, not commandments. Therefore, we shouldn't always trust our own emotions. In fact, I believe we should make a habit of questioning them.

Many people are taught to repress their emotions for various personal, social, or cultural reasons—particularly negative emotions. Sadly, to deny one's negative emotions is to deny many of the feedback mechanisms that help a person solve problems. As a result, many of these repressed individuals struggle to deal with problems throughout their lives. And if they can't solve problems, then they can't be happy. Remember, pain serves a purpose.

But then there are those people who overidentify with their emotions. Everything is justified for no other reason than they *felt* it. "Oh, I broke your windshield, but I was *really* mad; I couldn't help it." Or "I dropped out of school and moved to Alaska just because it *felt* right." Decision-making based on emotional intuition, without the aid of reason to keep it in line, pretty much always sucks. You know who bases their entire lives on their emotions? Three-year-old kids. And dogs. You know what else three-year-olds and dogs do? Shit on the carpet.

An obsession and overinvestment in emotion fails us for the simple reason that emotions never last. Whatever makes us happy today will no longer make us happy tomorrow, because our biology always needs something more. A fixation on happiness inevitably amounts to a never-ending pursuit of "something else"—a new house, a new relationship, another child, another pay raise. And despite all of our sweat and strain, we end up feeling eerily similar to how we started: inadequate.

Psychologists sometimes refer to this concept as the "hedonic treadmill": the idea that we're always working hard to change our life situation, but we actually never feel very different.

This is why our problems are recursive and unavoidable. The person you marry is the person you fight with. The house you buy is the house you repair. The dream job you take is the job you stress over. Everything comes with an inherent sacrifice—whatever makes us feel good will also inevitably make us feel bad. What we gain is also what we lose. What creates our positive experiences will define our negative experiences.

This is a difficult pill to swallow. We *like* the idea that there's some form of ultimate happiness that can be attained. We *like* the idea that we can alleviate all of our suffering permanently. We *like* the idea that we can feel fulfilled and satisfied with our lives forever.

But we cannot.

Choose Your Struggle

If I ask you, "What do you want out of life?" and you say something like, "I want to be happy and have a great family and a job I like," your response is so common and expected that it doesn't really mean anything.

Everybody enjoys what feels good. Everyone wants to live a carefree, happy, and easy life, to fall in love and have amazing sex and relationships, to look perfect and make money and be popular and well-respected and admired and a total baller to the point that people part like the Red Sea when they walk into the room.

Everybody wants that. It's easy to want that.

A more interesting question, a question that most people never consider, is, "What *pain* do you want in your life? What are you willing to struggle for?" Because that seems to be a greater determinant of how our lives turn out.

For example, most people want to get the corner office and make a boatload of money—but not many people want to suffer through sixty-hour workweeks, long commutes, obnoxious paperwork, and arbitrary corporate hierarchies to escape the confines of an infinite cubicle hell.

Most people want to have great sex and an awesome relationship, but not everyone is willing to go through the tough conversations, the awkward silences, the hurt feelings, and the emotional psychodrama to get there. And so they settle. They settle and wonder, "What if?" for years and years, until the question morphs from "What if?" into "What else?" And when the lawyers go home and the alimony check is in the mail, they say, "What for?" If not for their lowered standards and expectations twenty years prior, then what for?

Because happiness requires struggle. It grows from problems. Joy doesn't just sprout out of the ground like daisies and rainbows. Real, serious, lifelong fulfillment and meaning have to be earned through the choosing and managing of our struggles. Whether you suffer from anxiety or loneliness or obsessive-compulsive disorder or a dickhead boss who ruins half of your waking hours every day, the solution lies in the acceptance and active engagement of that negative experience—not the avoidance of it, not the salvation from it.

People want an amazing physique. But you don't end up with one unless you legitimately appreciate the pain and physical stress that come with living inside a gym for hour upon hour, unless you love calculating and calibrating the food you eat, planning your life out in tiny plate–sized portions.

People want to start their own business. But you don't end up a successful entrepreneur unless you find a way to appreciate the risk, the uncertainty, the repeated failures, the insane hours devoted to something that may earn absolutely nothing.

People want a partner, a spouse. But you don't end up attracting someone amazing without appreciating the emotional turbulence that comes with weathering rejections, building the sexual tension that never gets released, and staring blankly at a phone that never rings. It's part of the game of love. You can't win if you don't play.

What determines your success isn't, "What do you want to enjoy?" The relevant question is, "What pain do you want to sustain?" The path to happiness is a path full of shit-heaps and shame.

You have to choose something. You can't have a pain-free life. It can't all be roses and unicorns all the time. Pleasure is the easy question. And pretty much all of us have a similar answer.

The more interesting question is the pain. What is the pain that you want to sustain? That's the hard question that matters, the question that will actually get you somewhere. It's the question that can change a perspective, a life. It's what makes me, me, and you, you. It's what defines us and separates us and ultimately brings us together.

For most of my adolescence and young adulthood, I

fantasized about being a musician—a rock star, in particular. Any badass guitar song I heard, I would always close my eyes and envision myself up on stage, playing it to the screams of the crowd, people absolutely losing their minds to my sweet finger-noodling glory. This fantasy could keep me occupied for hours on end. For me, it was never a question of *if* I'd ever be up playing in front of screaming crowds, but *when*. I had it all planned out. I was simply biding my time before I could invest the proper amount of energy and effort into getting out there and making my mark. First I needed to finish school. Then I needed to make some extra money to buy gear. Then I needed to find enough free time to practice. Then I had to network and plan my first project. Then . . . and then nothing.

Despite my fantasizing about this for over half my lifetime, the reality never came to fruition. And it took me a long time and a lot of struggle to finally figure out why: *I didn't actually want it.*

I was in love with the result—the image of me on stage, people cheering, me rocking out, pouring my heart into what I was playing—but I wasn't in love with the process. And because of that, I failed at it. Repeatedly. Hell, I didn't even try hard enough to fail at it. I hardly tried at all. The daily drudgery of practicing, the logistics of finding a group and rehearsing, the pain of finding gigs and actually getting people to show up and give a shit, the broken strings, the blown tube amp, hauling forty pounds of gear to and from rehearsals with no car. It's a mountain of a dream and a mile-high climb to the top. And what it took me a long time to discover is that I didn't like to climb much. I just liked to imagine the summit.

The common cultural narratives would tell me that I somehow failed myself, that I'm a quitter or a loser, that I just didn't "have it," that I gave up on my dream and that maybe I let myself succumb to the pressures of society.

But the truth is far less interesting than any of these explanations. The truth is, I thought I wanted something, but it turns out I didn't. End of story.

I wanted the reward and not the struggle. I wanted the result and not the process. I was in love with not the fight but only the victory.

And life doesn't work that way.

Who you are is defined by what you're willing to struggle for. People who *enjoy* the struggles of a gym are the ones who run triathlons and have chiseled abs and can bench-press a small house. People who *enjoy* long workweeks and the politics of the corporate ladder are the ones who fly to the top of it. People who *enjoy* the stresses and uncertainties of the starving artist lifestyle are ultimately the ones who live it and make it.

This is not about willpower or grit. This is not another admonishment of "no pain, no gain." This is the most simple and basic component of life: our struggles determine our successes. Our problems birth our happiness, along with slightly better, slightly upgraded problems.

See: it's a never-ending upward spiral. And if you think at any point you're allowed to stop climbing, I'm afraid you're missing the point. Because the joy is in the climb itself.

You Are Not Special

I once knew a guy; we'll call him Jimmy.

Jimmy always had various business ventures going. On any given day, if you asked him what he was doing, he'd rattle off the name of some firm he was consulting with, or he'd describe a promising medical app he was looking for angel investors to fund, or he'd talk about some charity event he was supposed to be the keynote speaker for, or how he had an idea for a more efficient type of gas pump that was going to make him billions. The guy was always rolling, always on, and if you gave him an inch of conversational daylight, he'd pulverize you about how world-spinning his work was, how brilliant his latest ideas were, and he'd name-drop so much it felt like you were talking to a tabloid reporter.

Jimmy was all positivity all the time. Always pushing

himself, always working an angle—a real go-getter, whatever the fuck that means.

The catch was that Jimmy was also a total deadbeat—all talk and no walk. Stoned a majority of the time, and spending as much money in bars and fine restaurants as he did on his "business ideas," Jimmy was a professional leech, living off his family's hard-won money by spinning them as well as everybody else in the city on false ideas of future tech glory. Sure, sometimes he'd put in some token effort, or pick up the phone and cold-call some bigwig and name-drop until he ran out of names, but nothing ever actually happened. None of these "ventures" ever blossomed into anything.

Yet the guy kept this up for years, living off girlfriends and more and more distant relatives well into his late twenties. And the most screwed-up part was that Jimmy *felt good about it*. He had a delusional level of self-confidence. People who laughed at him or hung up on him were, in his mind, "missing the opportunity of their lives." People who called him out on his bogus business ideas were "too ignorant and inexperienced" to understand his genius. People who pointed out his deadbeat lifestyle were "jealous"; they were "haters" who envied his success.

Jimmy did make some money, although it was usually through the sketchiest of means, like selling another person's business idea as his own, or finagling a loan from someone, or worse, talking someone into giving him equity in their start-up. He actually occasionally talked people into paying him to do some public speaking. (About what, I can't even imagine.)

The worst part was that Jimmy *believed* his own bullshit. His delusion was so bulletproof, it was honestly hard to get mad at him, it was actually kind of amazing.

Sometime in the 1960s, developing "high self-esteem"— having positive thoughts and feelings about oneself— became all the rage in psychology. Research found that people who *thought* highly about themselves generally performed better and caused fewer problems. Many researchers and policymakers at the time came to believe that raising a population's self-esteem could lead to some tangible social benefits: lower crime, better academic records, greater employment, lower budget deficits. As a result, beginning in the next decade, the 1970s, self-esteem practices began to be taught to parents, emphasized by therapists, politicians, and teachers, and instituted into educational policy. Grade inflation, for example, was implemented to make low-achieving kids feel better about their lack of achievement. Participation awards and bogus trophies were invented for any number of mundane and expected activities. Kids were given inane homework assignments, like writing down all the reasons why they thought they were special, or the five things they liked most about themselves. Pastors and ministers told their congregations that they were each uniquely special in God's eyes, and were destined to excel and not be average. Business and motivational seminars cropped up chanting the same paradoxical mantra: every single one of us can be exceptional and massively successful.

But it's a generation later and the data is in: we're *not* all exceptional. It turns out that merely feeling good about yourself doesn't really mean anything unless you have a *good reason* to feel good about yourself. It turns out that adversity and failure are actually useful and even necessary for developing strong-minded and successful adults. It turns out that teaching people to believe they're exceptional and to feel good about themselves no matter what doesn't lead to a population full of Bill Gateses and Martin Luther Kings. It leads to a population full of Jimmys.

Jimmy, the delusional start-up founder. Jimmy, who smoked pot every day and had no real marketable skills other than talking himself up and believing it. Jimmy, the type of guy who yelled at his business partner for being "immature," and then maxed out the company credit card at Le Bernardin trying to impress some Russian model. Jimmy, who was quickly running out of aunts and uncles who could loan him more money.

Yes, that confident, high-self-esteem Jimmy. The Jimmy who spent so much time talking about how good he was that he forgot to, you know, actually do something.

The problem with the self-esteem movement is that it measured self-esteem by how positively people felt about themselves. But a true and accurate measurement of one's self-worth is how people feel about the *negative* aspects of themselves. If a person like Jimmy feels absolutely fucking great 99.9 percent of the time, despite his life falling apart around him, then how can that be a valid metric for a successful and happy life?

Jimmy is entitled. That is, he feels as though he deserves good things without actually earning them. He believes he should be able to be rich without actually working for it. He believes he should be liked and well-connected without actually helping anyone. He believes he should have an amazing lifestyle without actually sacrificing anything.

People like Jimmy become so fixated on feeling good about themselves that they manage to delude themselves into believing that they *are* accomplishing great things even when they're not. They believe they're the brilliant presenter on stage when actually they're making a fool of themselves. They believe they're the successful start-up founder when, in fact, they've never had a successful venture. They call themselves life coaches and charge money to help others, even though they're only twenty-five years old and haven't actually accomplished anything substantial in their lives.

Entitled people exude a delusional degree of self-confidence. This confidence can be alluring to others, at least for a little while. In some instances, the entitled person's delusional level of confidence can become contagious and help the people around the entitled person feel more confident in themselves too. Despite all of Jimmy's shenanigans, I have to admit that it *was* fun hanging out with him sometimes. You felt indestructible around him.

But the problem with entitlement is that it makes people *need* to feel good about themselves all the time, even at the expense of those around them. And because entitled people always need to feel good about themselves, they end up spending most of their time thinking about themselves. After all, it takes a lot of energy and work to convince yourself that your shit doesn't stink, especially when you've actually been living in a toilet.

Once people have developed the thought pattern to constantly construe what happens around them as self-aggrandizing, it's extremely hard to break them out of it. Any attempt to reason with them is seen as simply another "threat" to their superiority by another person who "can't handle" how smart/talented/good-looking/successful they are.

Entitlement closes in upon itself in a kind of narcissistic bubble, distorting anything and everything in such a way as to reinforce itself. People who feel entitled view every occurrence in their life as either an affirmation of, or a threat to, their own greatness. If something good happens to them, it's because of some amazing feat they accomplished. If something bad happens to them, it's because somebody is jealous and trying to bring them down a notch. Entitlement is impervious. People who are entitled delude themselves into whatever feeds their sense of superiority. They keep their mental facade standing at all costs, even if it sometimes requires being physically or emotionally abusive to those around them.

But entitlement is a failed strategy. It's just another high. It's *not* happiness.

The true measurement of self-worth is not how a person feels about her *positive* experiences, but rather how she feels about her *negative* experiences. A person like Jimmy hides from his problems by making up imagined successes for himself at every turn. And because he can't face his problems, no matter how good he feels about himself, he is weak.

A person who actually has a high self-worth is able to look at the negative parts of his character frankly—"Yes, sometimes I'm irresponsible with money," "Yes, sometimes I exaggerate my own successes," "Yes, I rely too much on others to support me and should be more self-reliant"— and then acts to improve upon them. But entitled people, because they are incapable of acknowledging their own problems openly and honestly, are incapable of improving their lives in any lasting or meaningful way. They are left chasing high after high and accumulate greater and greater levels of denial.

But eventually reality must hit, and the underlying problems will once again make themselves clear. It's just a question of when, and how painful it will be.

Things Fall Apart

I sat in my 9:00 A.M. biology class, arms cradling my head on my desk as I stared at the clock's second hand making laps, each tick syncopated with the teacher's dronings-on about chromosomes and mitosis. Like most thirteen-year-olds stuck in a stuffy, fluorescent classroom, I was bored.

A knock came on the door. Mr. Price, the school's assistant principal, stuck his head in. "Excuse me for interrupting. Mark, can you step outside with me for a moment? Oh, and bring your things with you."

Strange, I thought. Kids get sent to the principal, but the principal rarely gets sent to them. I gathered my things and stepped out.

The hallway was empty. Hundreds of beige lockers converged on the horizon. "Mark, can you take me to your locker, please?"

"Sure," I say, and slug myself down the hall, baggy jeans and moppy hair and oversized Pantera T-shirt and all.

We get to my locker. "Open it, please," Mr. Price says; so I do. He steps in front of me and gathers my coat, my gym bag, my backpack—all of the locker's contents, minus a few notebooks and pencils. He starts walking away. "Come with me, please," he says, without looking back. I start to get an uneasy feeling.

I follow him to his office, where he asks me to sit down. He closes the door and locks it. He goes over to the window and adjusts the blinds to block the view from outside. My palms begin to sweat. This is *not* a normal principal visit.

Mr. Price sits down and quietly rummages through my things, checking pockets, unzipping zippers, shaking out my gym clothes and placing them on the floor.

Without looking up at me, Mr. Price asks, "Do you know what I'm looking for, Mark?"

"No," I say.

"Drugs."

The word shocks me into nervous attention.

"D-d-drugs?" I stammer. "What kind?"

He looks at me sternly. "I don't know; what kind do you

have?" He opens one of my binders and checks the small pockets meant for pens.

My sweat blossoms like a fungal growth. It spreads from my palms to my arms and now my neck. My temples pulsate as blood floods my brain and face. Like most thirteen-year-olds freshly accused of possessing narcotics and bringing them to school, I want to run away and hide.

"I don't know what you're talking about," I protest, the words sounding far meeker than I'd like. I feel as if I should be sounding confident in myself right now. Or maybe not. Maybe I should be scared. Do liars sound more scared or confident? Because however they sound, I want to sound the opposite. Instead, my lack of confidence compounds, unconfidence about my sounding unconfident making me more unconfident. That fucking Feedback Loop from Hell.

"We'll see about that," he says, turning his attention to my backpack, which seemingly has one hundred pockets. Each is loaded with its own silly teen desiderata—colored pens, old notes passed in class, early-nineties CDs with cracked cases, dried-up markers, an old sketchpad with half its pages missing, dust and lint and crap accumulated during a maddeningly circuitous middle school existence.

My sweat must be pumping at the speed of light, because time extends itself and dilates such that what is mere seconds on that 9:00 A.M. second-period biology clock now feels like Paleolithic eons, and I'm growing up and dying every minute. Just me and Mr. Price and my bottomless backpack.

Somewhere around the Mesolithic Age, Mr. Price

finishes searching the backpack. Having found nothing, he seems flustered. He turns the pack upside down and lets all of my crap crash onto his office floor. He's now sweating as profusely as I am, except in place of my terror, there is his anger.

"No drugs today, eh?" He tries to sound casual.

"Nope." So do I.

He spreads my stuff out, separating each item and coagulating them into little piles beside my gym gear. My coat and backpack now lie empty and lifeless on his lap. He sighs and stares at the wall. Like most thirteen-year-olds locked in an office with a man angrily throwing their shit all over the floor, I want to cry.

Mr. Price scans the contents organized on the floor. Nothing illicit or illegal, no narcotics, not even anything against school policy. He sighs and then throws the coat and backpack on the floor too. He bends over and puts his elbows on his knees, making his face level with mine.

"Mark, I'm going to give you one last chance to be honest with me. If you are honest, this will turn out much better for you. If it turns out you're lying, then it's going to be much worse."

As if on cue, I gulp.

"Now tell me the truth," Mr. Price demands. "Did you bring drugs to school today?"

Fighting back tears, screams clawing at my throat, I stare my tormentor in the face and, in a pleading voice, dying to be relieved of its adolescent horrors, I say, "No, I don't have any drugs. I have no idea what you're talking about."

"Okay," he says, signaling surrender. "I guess you can collect your things and go."

He takes one last, longing gaze at my deflated backpack, lying like a broken promise there on his office floor. He casually puts one foot down on the pack, stomping lightly, a last-ditch effort. I anxiously wait for him to get up and leave so I can get on with my life and forget this whole nightmare.

But his foot stops on something. "What is this?" he asks, tapping with his foot.

"What is what?" I say.

"There's still something in here." He picks up the bag and starts feeling around the bottom of it. For me the room gets fuzzy; everything goes wobbly.

When I was young, I was smart. I was friendly. But I was also a shithead. I mean that in the most loving way possible. I was a rebellious, lying little shithead. Angry and full of resentment. When I was twelve, I hacked my house's security system with refrigerator magnets so I could sneak out undetected in the middle of the night. My friend and I would put his mom's car in neutral and push it into the street so we could drive around without waking her up. I would write papers about abortion because I knew my English teacher was a hardcore conservative Christian. Another friend and I stole cigarettes from his mom and sold them to kids out behind the school.

And I also cut a secret compartment into the bottom of my backpack to hide my marijuana.

That was the same hidden compartment Mr. Price found after stepping on the drugs I was hiding. I had been lying. And, as promised, Mr. Price didn't go easy on me. A few hours later, like most thirteen-year-olds handcuffed in the back of a police car, I thought my life was over.

And I was kind of right, in a way. My parents quarantined me at home. I was to have no friends for the foreseeable future. Having been expelled from school, I was to be homeschooled for the rest of the year. My mom made me get a haircut and threw out all of my Marilyn Manson and Metallica shirts (which, for an adolescent in 1998, was tantamount to being sentenced to death by lameness). My dad dragged me to his office with him in the mornings and made me file papers for hours on end. Once homeschooling was over, I was enrolled in a small, private Christian school, where—and this may not surprise you—I didn't exactly fit in.

And just when I had finally cleaned up my act and turned in my assignments and learned the value of good clerical responsibility, my parents decided to get divorced.

I tell you all of this only to point out that my adolescence sucked donkey balls. I lost all of my friends, my community, my legal rights, and my family within the span of about nine months. My therapist in my twenties would later call this "some real traumatic shit," and I would spend the next decade-and-change working on unraveling it and becoming less of a self-absorbed, entitled little prick.

The problem with my home life back then was not all of the horrible things that were said or done; rather, it was all of the horrible things that needed to be said and done but weren't. My family stonewalls the way Warren Buffett makes money or Jenna Jameson fucks: we're champions at it. The house could have been burning down around us and it would have been met with, "Oh no, everything's fine. A tad warm in here, perhaps—but really, everything's fine."

When my parents got divorced, there were no broken dishes, no slammed doors, no screaming arguments about who fucked whom. Once they had reassured my brother and me that it wasn't our fault, we had a Q&A session—yes, you read that right—about the logistics of the new living arrangements. Not a tear was shed. Not a voice was raised. The closest peek my brother and I got into our parents' unraveling emotional lives was hearing, "Nobody cheated on anybody." Oh, that's nice. It was a tad warm in the room, but really, everything was fine.

My parents are good people. I don't blame them for any of this (not anymore, at least). And I love them very much. They have their own stories and their own journeys and their own problems, just as all parents do. And just as all of *their* parents do, and so on. And like all parents, my parents, with the best of intentions, imparted some of their problems to me, as I probably will to my kids.

When "real traumatic shit" like this happens in our lives, we begin to unconsciously feel as though we have problems that we're incapable of ever solving. And this assumed inability to solve our problems causes us to feel miserable and helpless.

But it also causes something else to happen. If we have problems that are unsolvable, our unconscious figures that we're either uniquely special or uniquely defective in some way. That we're somehow unlike everyone else and that the rules must be different for us.

Put simply: we become entitled.

The pain from my adolescence led me down a road of entitlement that lasted through much of my early adulthood. Whereas Jimmy's entitlement played out in the business world, where he pretended to be a huge success, my entitlement played out in my relationships, particularly with women. My trauma had revolved around intimacy and acceptance, so I felt a constant need to overcompensate, to prove to myself that I was loved and accepted at all times. And as a result, I soon took to chasing women the same way a cocaine addict takes to a snowman made out of cocaine: I made sweet love to it, and then promptly suffocated myself in it.

I became a player—an immature, selfish, albeit sometimes charming player. And I strung up a long series of superficial and unhealthy relationships for the better part of a decade.

It wasn't so much the sex I craved, although the sex was fun. It was the validation. I was wanted; I was loved; for the first time since I could remember, I was *worthy*. My craving for validation quickly fed into a mental habit of self-aggrandizing and overindulgence. I felt entitled to say or do whatever I wanted, to break people's trust, to ignore people's feelings, and then justify it later with shitty, half-assed apologies.

While this period certainly had its moments of fun and excitement, and I met some wonderful women, my life was more or less a wreck the whole time. I was often unemployed, living on friends' couches or with my mom, drinking way more than I should have been, alienating a number of friends—and when I did meet a woman I really liked, my self-absorption quickly torpedoed everything.

The deeper the pain, the more helpless we feel against our problems, and the more entitlement we adopt to compensate for those problems. This entitlement plays out in one of two ways:

1. I'm awesome and the rest of you all suck, so I deserve special treatment.
2. I suck and the rest of you are all awesome, so I deserve special treatment.

Opposite mindset on the outside, but the same selfish creamy core in the middle. In fact, you will often see entitled people flip back and forth between the two. Either they're on top of the world or the world is on top of them, depending on the day of the week, or how well they're doing with their particular addiction at that moment.

Most people correctly identify a person like Jimmy as a raging narcissistic ass-hat. That's because he's pretty blatant in his delusionally high self-regard. What most people don't correctly identify as entitlement are those people who perpetually feel as though they're inferior and unworthy of the world.

Because construing everything in life so as to make yourself out to be constantly victimized requires just as much selfishness as the opposite. It takes just as much energy and delusional self-aggrandizement to maintain the belief that one has insurmountable problems as that one has no problems at all.

The truth is that there's no such thing as a personal problem. If you've got a problem, chances are millions of other people have had it in the past, have it now, and are going to have it in the future. Likely people you know too. That doesn't minimize the problem or mean that it shouldn't hurt. It doesn't mean you aren't legitimately a victim in some circumstances.

It just means that you're not special.

Often, it's this realization—that you and your problems are actually *not* privileged in their severity or pain—that is the first and most important step toward solving them.

But for some reason, it appears that more and more people, particularly young people, are forgetting this. Numerous professors and educators have noted a lack of emotional resilience and an excess of selfish demands in today's young people. It's not uncommon now for books to be removed from a class's curriculum for no other reason than that they made someone feel bad. Speakers and professors are shouted down and banned from campuses for infractions as simple as suggesting that maybe some Halloween costumes really aren't that offensive. School counselors note that more students than ever are exhibiting severe signs of emotional distress over what are otherwise run-of-the-mill daily college experiences, such as an argument with a roommate, or getting a low grade in a class.

It's strange that in an age when we are more connected than ever, entitlement seems to be at an all-time high. Something about recent technology seems to allow our insecurities to run amok like never before. The more freedom we're given to express ourselves, the more we want to be free of having to deal with anyone who may disagree with us or upset us. The more exposed we are to opposing viewpoints, the more we seem to get upset that those other viewpoints exist. The easier and more problem-free our lives become, the more we seem to feel entitled for them to get even better.

The benefits of the Internet and social media are unquestionably fantastic. In many ways, this is the best time in history to be alive. But perhaps these technologies are having some unintended social side effects. Perhaps these same technologies that have liberated and educated so many are simultaneously enabling people's sense of entitlement more than ever before.

The Tyranny of Exceptionalism

Most of us are pretty average at most things we do. Even if you're exceptional at one thing, chances are you're average or below average at most other things. That's just the nature of life. To become truly great at something, you have to dedicate shit-tons of time and energy to it. And because we all have limited time and energy, few of us ever become truly exceptional at more than one thing, if anything at all.

We can then say that it's a statistical improbability that any single person will be an extraordinary performer in all areas of life, or even in many areas of their life. Brilliant businesspeople are often fuckups in their personal lives. Extraordinary athletes are often shallow and as dumb as a lobotomized rock. Many celebrities are probably just as clueless about life as the people who gawk at them and follow their every move.

We're all, for the most part, pretty average people. But it's the extremes that get all of the publicity. We kind of know this already, but we rarely think and/or talk about it, and we certainly never discuss why this could be a problem.

Having the Internet, Google, Facebook, YouTube, and access to five hundred–plus channels of television is amazing. But our attention is limited. There's no way we can process the tidal waves of information flowing past us constantly. Therefore, the only zeroes and ones that break through and catch our attention are the truly exceptional pieces of information—those in the 99.999th percentile.

All day, every day, we are flooded with the truly extraordinary. The best of the best. The worst of the worst. The greatest physical feats. The funniest jokes. The most upsetting news. The scariest threats. Nonstop.

Our lives today are filled with information from the extremes of the bell curve of human experience, because in the media business that's what gets eyeballs, and eyeballs bring dollars. That's the bottom line. Yet the vast majority of life resides in the humdrum middle. The vast majority of life is *un*extraordinary, indeed quite average.

This flood of extreme information has conditioned us to believe that exceptionalism is the new normal. And because we're all quite average most of the time, the deluge of exceptional information drives us to feel pretty damn insecure and desperate, because clearly we are somehow not good enough. So more and more we feel the need to compensate through entitlement and addiction. We cope the only way we know how: either through self-aggrandizing or through other-aggrandizing.

Some of us do this by cooking up get-rich-quick schemes. Others do it by taking off across the world to save starving babies in Africa. Others do it by excelling in school and winning every award. Others do it by shooting up a school. Others do it by trying to have sex with anything that talks and breathes.

This ties in to the growing culture of entitlement that I talked about earlier. Millennials often get blamed for this cultural shift, but that's likely because millennials are the most plugged-in and visible generation. In fact, the tendency toward entitlement is apparent across all of society. And I believe it's linked to mass-media-driven exceptionalism.

The problem is that the pervasiveness of technology and mass marketing is screwing up a lot of people's expectations for themselves. The inundation of the exceptional makes people feel worse about themselves, makes them feel that they need to be more extreme, more radical, and more self-assured to get noticed or even matter.

When I was a young man, my insecurities around intimacy were exacerbated by all the ridiculous narratives of masculinity circulating throughout pop culture. And those same narratives are *still* circulating: to be a cool guy, you have to party like a rock star; to be respected, you have to be admired by women; sex is the most valuable thing a man can attain, and it's worth sacrificing anything (including your own dignity) to get it.

This constant stream of unrealistic media dogpiles onto our existing feelings of insecurity, by overexposing us to the unrealistic standards we fail to live up to. Not only do we feel subjected to unsolvable problems, but we feel like losers because a simple Google search shows us thousands of people without those same problems.

Technology has solved old economic problems by giving us new psychological problems. The Internet has not just open-sourced information; it has also open-sourced insecurity, self-doubt, and shame.

B-b-b-but, If I'm Not Going to Be Special or Extraordinary, What's the Point?

It has become an accepted part of our culture today to believe that we are *all* destined to do something truly extraordinary. Celebrities say it. Business tycoons say it. Politicians say it. Even Oprah says it (so it must be true). Each and every one of us can be extraordinary. We all *deserve* greatness.

The fact that this statement is inherently contradictory—after all, if *everyone* were extraordinary, then by definition *no one* would be extraordinary—is missed by most people. And instead of questioning what we actually deserve or don't deserve, we eat the message up and ask for more.

Being "average" has become the new standard of failure. The worst thing you can be is in the middle of the pack, the middle of the bell curve. When a culture's standard of success is to "be extraordinary," it then becomes better to be at the extreme low end of the bell curve than to be in the middle, because at least there you're still special and deserve attention. Many people choose this strategy: to prove to everyone that they are the most miserable, or the most oppressed, or the most victimized.

A lot of people are afraid to accept mediocrity because they believe that if they accept it, they'll never achieve anything, never improve, and that their life won't matter.

This sort of thinking is dangerous. Once you accept the premise that a life is worthwhile only if it is truly notable and great, then you basically accept the fact that most of the human population (including yourself) sucks and is worthless. And this mindset can quickly turn dangerous, to both yourself and others.

The rare people who do become truly exceptional at something do so not because they believe they're exceptional. On the contrary, they become amazing because they're obsessed with improvement. And that obsession with improvement stems from an unerring belief that they are, in fact, not that great at all. It's *anti*-entitlement. People who become great at something become great because they understand that they're not already great— they are mediocre, they are average—and that they could be so much better.

All of this "every person can be extraordinary and achieve greatness" stuff is basically just jerking off your ego. It's a message that tastes good going down, but in reality is nothing more than empty calories that make you emotionally fat and bloated, the proverbial Big Mac for your heart and your brain.

The ticket to emotional health, like that to physical health, comes from eating your veggies—that is, accepting the bland and mundane truths of life: truths such as "Your actions actually don't matter *that much* in the grand scheme of things" and "The vast majority of your life will be boring and not noteworthy, and that's okay." This vegetable course will taste bad at first. Very bad. You will avoid accepting it.

But once ingested, your body will wake up feeling more potent and more alive. After all, that constant pressure to be something amazing, to be the next big thing, will be lifted off your back. The stress and anxiety of always feeling inadequate and constantly needing to prove yourself will dissipate. And the knowledge and acceptance of your own mundane existence will actually free you to accomplish what you truly wish to accomplish, without judgment or lofty expectations.

You will have a growing appreciation for life's basic experiences: the pleasures of simple friendship, creating something, helping a person in need, reading a good book, laughing with someone you care about.

Sounds boring, doesn't it? That's because these things are ordinary. But maybe they're ordinary for a reason: because they are what *actually* matters.

4

The Value of Suffering

I n the closing months of 1944, after almost a decade of war, the tide was turning against Japan. Their economy was floundering, their military overstretched across half of Asia, and the territories they had won throughout the Pacific were now toppling like dominoes to U.S. forces. Defeat seemed inevitable.

On December 26, 1944, Second Lieutenant Hiroo Onoda of the Japanese Imperial Army was deployed to the small island of Lubang in the Philippines. His orders were to slow the United States' progress as much as possible, to stand and fight at all costs, and to never surrender. Both he and his commander knew it was essentially a suicide mission.

In February 1945, the Americans arrived on Lubang and took the island with overwhelming force. Within days, most of the Japanese soldiers had either surrendered or been killed, but Onoda and three of his men managed to hide in the jungle. From there, they began a guerrilla warfare campaign against the U.S. forces and the local population, attacking supply lines, shooting at stray soldiers, and interfering with the American forces in any way that they could.

That August, half a year later, the United States dropped atomic bombs on the cities of Hiroshima and Nagasaki. Japan surrendered, and the deadliest war in human history came to its dramatic conclusion.

However, thousands of Japanese soldiers were still scattered among the Pacific isles, and most, like Onoda, were hiding in the jungle, unaware that the war was over. These holdouts continued to fight and pillage as they had before. This was a real problem for rebuilding eastern Asia after the war, and the governments agreed something must be done.

The U.S. military, in conjunction with the Japanese government, dropped thousands of leaflets throughout the Pacific region, announcing that the war was over and it was time for everyone to go home. Onoda and his men, like many others, found and read these leaflets, but unlike most of the others, Onoda decided that they were fake, a trap set by the American forces to get the guerrilla fighters to show themselves. Onoda burned the leaflets, and he and his men stayed hidden and continued to fight.

Five years went by. The leaflets had stopped, and most of the American forces had long since gone home. The local population on Lubang attempted to return to their normal lives of farming and fishing. Yet there were Hiroo Onoda and his merry men, still shooting at the farmers, burning their crops, stealing their livestock, and murdering locals who wandered too far into the jungle. The Philippine government then took to drawing up new flyers and spreading them out across the jungle. Come out, they said. The war is over. You lost.

But these, too, were ignored.

In 1952, the Japanese government made one final effort to draw the last remaining soldiers out of hiding throughout the Pacific. This time, letters and pictures from the missing soldiers' families were air-dropped, along with a personal note from the emperor himself. Once again, Onoda refused to believe that the information was real. Once again, he believed the airdrop to be a trick by the Americans. Once again, he and his men stood and continued to fight.

Another few years went by and the Philippine locals, sick of being terrorized, finally armed themselves and began firing back. By 1959, one of Onoda's companions had surrendered, and another had been killed. Then, a decade later, Onoda's last companion, a man called Kozuka, was killed in a shootout with the local police while he was burning rice fields—*still* waging war against the local population a full quarter-century after the end of World War II!

Onoda, having now spent more than half of his life in the jungles of Lubang, was all alone.

In 1972, the news of Kozuka's death reached Japan and caused a stir. The Japanese people thought the last of the soldiers from the war had come home years earlier. The Japanese media began to wonder: if Kozuka had still been on Lubang until 1972, then perhaps Onoda himself, the last known Japanese holdout from World War II, might still be alive as well. That year, both the Japanese and Philippine governments sent search parties to look for the enigmatic second lieutenant, now part myth, part hero, and part ghost.

They found nothing.

As the months progressed, the story of Lieutenant Onoda morphed into something of an urban legend in Japan—the war hero who sounded too insane to actually exist. Many romanticized him. Others criticized him. Others thought he was the stuff of fairy tale, invented by those who still wanted to believe in a Japan that had disappeared long ago.

It was around this time that a young man named Norio Suzuki first heard of Onoda. Suzuki was an adventurer, an explorer, and a bit of a hippie. Born after the war ended, he had dropped out of school and spent four years hitchhiking his way across Asia, the Middle East, and Africa, sleeping on park benches, in stranger's cars, in jail cells, and under the stars. He volunteered on farms for food, and donated blood to pay for places to stay. He was a free spirit, and perhaps a little bit nuts.

In 1972, Suzuki needed another adventure. He had returned to Japan after his travels and found the strict cultural norms and social hierarchy to be stifling. He hated school. He couldn't hold down a job. He wanted to be back on the road, back on his own again.

For Suzuki, the legend of Hiroo Onoda came as the answer to his problems. It was a new and worthy adventure for him to pursue. Suzuki believed that *he* would be the one who would find Onoda. Sure, search parties conducted by the Japanese, Philippine, and American governments had not been able to find Onoda; local police forces had been scavenging the jungle for almost thirty years with no luck; thousands of leaflets had met with no response—but fuck it, this deadbeat, college-dropout hippie was going to be the one to find him.

Unarmed and untrained for any sort of reconnaissance or tactical warfare, Suzuki traveled to Lubang and began wandering around the jungle all by himself. His strategy: scream Onoda's name really loudly and tell him that the emperor was worried about him.

He found Onoda in four days.

Suzuki stayed with Onoda in the jungle for some time. Onoda had been alone by that point for over a year, and once found by Suzuki he welcomed the companionship and was desperate to learn what had been happening in the outside world from a Japanese source he could trust. The two men became sorta-kinda friends.

Suzuki asked Onoda why he had stayed and continued to fight. Onoda said it was simple: he had been given the order to "never surrender," so he stayed. For nearly thirty years he had simply been following an order. Onoda then asked Suzuki why a "hippie boy" like himself came looking for him. Suzuki said that he'd left Japan in search of three things: "Lieutenant Onoda, a panda bear, and the Abominable Snowman, in that order."

The two men had been brought together under the most

curious of circumstances: two well-intentioned adventurers chasing false visions of glory, like a real-life Japanese Don Quixote and Sancho Panza, stuck together in the damp recesses of a Philippine jungle, both imagining themselves heroes, despite both being alone with nothing, doing nothing. Onoda had already by then given up most of his life to a phantom war. Suzuki would give his up too. Having already found Hiroo Onoda and the panda bear, he would die a few years later in the Himalayas, still in search of the Abominable Snowman.

Humans often choose to dedicate large portions of their lives to seemingly useless or destructive causes. On the surface, these causes make no sense. It's hard to imagine how Onoda could have been happy on that island for those thirty years—living off insects and rodents, sleeping in the dirt, murdering civilians decade after decade. Or why Suzuki trekked off to his own death, with no money, no companions, and no purpose other than to chase an imaginary Yeti.

Yet, later in his life, Onoda said he regretted nothing. He claimed that he was proud of his choices and his time on Lubang. He said that it had been an honor to devote a sizable portion of his life in service to a nonexistent empire. Suzuki, had he survived, likely would have said something similar: that he was doing exactly what he was meant to do, that he regretted nothing.

These men both chose how they wished to suffer. Hiroo Onoda chose to suffer for loyalty to a dead empire. Suzuki chose to suffer for adventure, no matter how ill-advised. To both men, their suffering *meant* something; it fulfilled some greater cause. And because it meant something, they were able to endure it, or perhaps even enjoy it.

If suffering is inevitable, if our problems in life are unavoidable, then the question we should be asking is not "How do I stop suffering?" but "*Why* am I suffering—for what purpose?"

Hiroo Onoda returned to Japan in 1974 and became a kind of celebrity in his home country. He was shuttled around from talk show to radio station; politicians clamored to shake his hand; he published a book and was even offered a large sum of money by the government.

But what he found when he returned to Japan horrified him: a consumerist, capitalist, superficial culture that had lost all of the traditions of honor and sacrifice upon which his generation had been raised.

Onoda tried to use his sudden celebrity to espouse the values of Old Japan, but he was tone-deaf to this new society. He was seen more as a showpiece than as a serious cultural thinker—a Japanese man who had emerged from a time capsule for all to marvel at, like a relic in a museum.

And in the irony of ironies, Onoda became far more depressed than he'd ever been in the jungle for all those years. At least in the jungle his life had stood for something; it had meant something. That had made his suffering endurable, indeed even a little bit desirable. But back in Japan, in what he considered to be a vacuous nation full of hippies and loose women in Western clothing, he was confronted with the unavoidable truth: that his fighting had meant nothing. The Japan he had lived and fought for no longer existed. And the weight of this realization pierced him in a way that no bullet ever had. Because his suffering had meant nothing, it suddenly became realized and true: thirty years wasted.

And so, in 1980, Onoda packed up and moved to Brazil, where he remained until he died.

The Self-Awareness Onion

Self-awareness is like an onion. There are multiple layers to it, and the more you peel them back, the more likely you're going to start crying at inappropriate times.

Let's say the first layer of the self-awareness onion is a simple understanding of one's emotions. "This is when I feel happy." "This makes me feel sad." "This gives me hope."

Unfortunately, there are many people who suck at even this most basic level of self-awareness. I know because I'm one of them. My wife and I sometimes have a fun back-and-forth that goes something like this:

> HER. What's wrong?
> ME. Nothing's wrong. Nothing at all.
> HER. No, something's wrong. Tell me.
> ME. I'm fine. Really.
> HER. Are you sure? You look upset.
> ME, *with nervous laughter.* Really? No, I'm okay, seriously.

[*Thirty minutes later . . .*]

ME. . . . And that's why I'm so fucking pissed off! He just acts as if I don't exist half the time.

We all have emotional blind spots. Often they have to do with the emotions that we were taught were inappropriate growing up. It takes years of practice and effort to get good at identifying blind spots in ourselves and then expressing the affected emotions appropriately. But this task is hugely important, and worth the effort.

The second layer of the self-awareness onion is an ability to ask *why* we feel certain emotions.

These *why* questions are difficult and often take months or even years to answer consistently and accurately. Most people need to go to some sort of therapist just to hear these questions asked for the first time. Such questions are important because they illuminate what we consider success or failure. Why do you feel angry? Is it because you failed to achieve some goal? Why do you feel lethargic and uninspired? Is it because you don't think you're good enough?

This layer of questioning helps us understand the root cause of the emotions that overwhelm us. Once we understand that root cause, we can ideally do something to change it.

But there's another, even deeper level of the self-awareness onion. And that one is full of fucking tears. The third level is our personal values: *Why* do I consider this to be success/failure? How am I choosing to measure myself? By what standard am I judging myself and everyone around me?

This level, which takes constant questioning and effort, is incredibly difficult to reach. But it's the most important, because our values determine the nature of our problems, and the nature of our problems determines the quality of our lives.

Values underlie everything we are and do. If what we value is unhelpful, if what we consider success/failure is poorly chosen, then everything based upon those values— the thoughts, the emotions, the day-to-day feelings—will all be out of whack. Everything we think and feel about a situation ultimately comes back to how valuable we perceive it to be.

Most people are horrible at answering these *why* questions accurately, and this prevents them from achieving a deeper knowledge of their own values. Sure, they may *say* they value honesty and a true friend, but then they turn around and lie about you behind your back to make themselves feel better. People may perceive that they feel lonely. But when they ask themselves *why* they feel lonely, they tend to come up with a way to blame others—everyone else is mean, or no one is cool or smart enough to understand them—and thus they further avoid their problem instead of seeking to solve it.

For many people this passes as self-awareness. And yet, if they were able to go deeper and look at their underlying values, they would see that their original analysis was based on avoiding responsibility for their own problem, rather than accurately identifying the problem. They would see

that their decisions were based on chasing highs, not generating true happiness.

Most self-help gurus ignore this deeper level of self-
awareness as well. They take people who are miserable because they want to be rich, and then give them all sorts of
advice on how to make more money, all the while ignoring
important values-based questions: *Why* do they feel such
a need to be rich in the first place? How are they choosing
to measure success/failure for themselves? Is it not perhaps
some particular value that's the root cause of their unhappiness, and not the fact that they don't drive a Bentley yet?

Much of the advice out there operates at a shallow level
of simply trying to make people feel good in the short term,
while the real long-term problems never get solved. People's
perceptions and feelings may change, but the underlying
values, and the metrics by which those values are assessed,
stay the same. This is not real progress. This is just another
way to achieve more highs.

Honest self-questioning is difficult. It requires asking
yourself simple questions that are uncomfortable to answer. In fact, in my experience, the more uncomfortable the
answer, the more likely it is to be true.

Take a moment and think of something that's really
bugging you. Now ask yourself *why* it bugs you. Chances
are the answer will involve a failure of some sort. Then take
that failure and ask why it seems "true" to you. What if that
failure wasn't really a failure? What if you've been looking
at it the wrong way?

A recent example from my own life:

"It bugs me that my brother doesn't return my texts or
emails."
Why?
"Because it feels like he doesn't give a shit about me."
Why does this seem true?
"Because if he wanted to have a relationship with me,
he would take ten seconds out of his day to interact
with me."
*Why does his lack of relationship with you feel like a
failure?*
"Because we're brothers; we're supposed to have a good
relationship!"

Two things are operating here: a value that I hold dear,
and a metric that I use to assess progress toward that value.
My value: brothers are supposed to have a good relationship
with one another. My metric: being in contact by phone or
email—this is how I measure my success as a brother. By
holding on to this metric, I make myself feel like a failure,
which occasionally ruins my Saturday mornings.

We could dig even deeper, by repeating the process:

Why are brothers supposed to have a good relationship?
"Because they're family, and family are supposed to be
close!"
Why does that seem true?

"Because your family is supposed to matter to you
more than anyone else!"
Why does that seem true?
"Because being close with your family is 'normal' and
'healthy,' and I don't have that."

In this exchange I'm clear about my underlying value—
having a good relationship with my brother—but I'm still
struggling with my metric. I've given it another name, "close-
ness," but the metric hasn't really changed: I'm still judging
myself as a brother based on frequency of contact—and
comparing myself, using that metric, against other people I
know. Everyone else (or so it seems) has a close relationship
with their family members, and I don't. So obviously there
must be something wrong with me.

But what if I'm choosing a poor metric for myself and
my life? What else could be true that I'm not considering?
Well, perhaps I don't need to be *close* to my brother to have
that good relationship that I *value*. Perhaps there just needs
to be some mutual respect (which there is). Or maybe mutual trust is what to look for (and it's there). Perhaps *these*
metrics would be better assessments of brotherhood than
how many text messages he and I exchange.

This clearly makes sense; it feels true for me. But it still
fucking hurts that my brother and I aren't close. And there's
no positive way to spin it. There's no secret way to glorify
myself through this knowledge. Sometimes brothers—even
brothers who love each other—don't have close relationships,

and that's fine. It is hard to accept at first, but that's fine. What is objectively true about your situation is not as important as how you come to see the situation, how you choose to measure it and value it. Problems may be inevitable, but the *meaning* of each problem is not. We get to control what our problems mean based on how we choose to think about them, the standard by which we choose to measure them.

Rock Star Problems

In 1983, a talented young guitarist was kicked out of his band in the worst possible way. The band had just been signed to a record deal, and they were about to record their first album. But a couple days before recording began, the band showed the guitarist the door—no warning, no discussion, no dramatic blowout; they literally woke him up one day by handing him a bus ticket home.

As he sat on the bus back to Los Angeles from New York, the guitarist kept asking himself: How did this happen? What did I do wrong? What will I do now? Record contracts didn't exactly fall out of the sky, especially for raucous, upstart metal bands. Had he missed his one and only shot?

But by the time the bus hit L.A., the guitarist had gotten over his self-pity and had vowed to start a new band. He decided that this new band would be so successful that his old band would forever regret their decision. He would become so famous that they would be subjected to decades of seeing him on TV, hearing him on the radio, seeing posters of him in the streets and pictures of him in magazines. They'd be flipping burgers somewhere, loading vans from their shitty club gigs, fat and drunk with their ugly wives, and he'd be rocking out in front of stadium crowds live on television. He'd bathe in the tears of his betrayers, each tear wiped dry by a crisp, clean hundred-dollar bill.

And so the guitarist worked as if possessed by a musical demon. He spent months recruiting the best musicians he could find—far better musicians than his previous bandmates. He wrote dozens of songs and practiced religiously. His seething anger fueled his ambition; revenge became his muse. Within a couple years, his new band had signed a record deal of their own, and a year after that, their first record would go gold.

The guitarist's name was Dave Mustaine, and the new band he formed was the legendary heavy-metal band Megadeth. Megadeth would go on to sell over 25 million albums and tour the world many times over. Today, Mustaine is considered one of the most brilliant and influential musicians in the history of heavy-metal music.

Unfortunately, the band he was kicked out of was Metallica, which has sold over 180 million albums worldwide. Metallica is considered by many to be one of the greatest rock bands of all time.

And because of this, in a rare intimate interview in 2003, a tearful Mustaine admitted that he couldn't help but *still* consider himself a failure. Despite all that he had accomplished, in his mind he would always be the guy who got kicked out of Metallica.

We're apes. We think we're all sophisticated with our toaster ovens and designer footwear, but we're just a bunch of finely ornamented apes. And because we are apes, we instinctually measure ourselves against others and vie for status. The question is not *whether* we evaluate ourselves against others; rather, the question is *by what standard* do we measure ourselves?

Dave Mustaine, whether he realized it or not, chose to measure himself by whether he was more successful and popular than Metallica. The experience of getting thrown out of his former band was so painful for him that he adopted "success relative to Metallica" as the metric by which to measure himself and his music career.

Despite taking a horrible event in his life and making something positive out of it, as Mustaine did with Megadeth, his choice to hold on to Metallica's success as his life-defining metric continued to hurt him decades later. Despite all the money and the fans and the accolades, he still considered himself a failure.

Now, you and I may look at Dave Mustaine's situation and laugh. Here's this guy with millions of dollars, hundreds of thousands of adoring fans, a career doing the thing he loves best, and *still* he's getting all weepy-eyed that his rock star buddies from twenty years ago are way more famous than he is.

This is because you and I have different values than Mustaine does, and we measure ourselves by different metrics. Our metrics are probably more like "I don't want to work a job for a boss I hate," or "I'd like to earn enough money to send my kid to a good school," or "I'd be happy to not wake up in a drainage ditch." And by these metrics,

Mustaine is wildly, unimaginably successful. But by *his* metric, "Be more popular and successful than Metallica," he's a failure.

Our values determine the metrics by which we measure ourselves and everyone else. Onoda's value of loyalty to the Japanese empire is what sustained him on Lubang for almost thirty years. But this same value is also what made him miserable upon his return to Japan. Mustaine's metric of being better than Metallica likely helped him launch an incredibly successful music career. But that same metric later tortured him in spite of his success.

If you want to change how you see your problems, you have to change what you value and/or how you measure failure/success.

As an example, let's look at another musician who got kicked out of another band. His story eerily echoes that of Dave Mustaine, although it happened two decades earlier.

It was 1962 and there was a buzz around an up-and-coming band from Liverpool, England. This band had funny haircuts and an even funnier name, but their music was undeniably good, and the record industry was finally taking notice.

There was John, the lead singer and songwriter; Paul, the boyish-faced romantic bass player; George, the rebellious lead guitar player. And then there was the drummer.

He was considered the best-looking of the bunch—the girls all went wild for him, and it was his face that began to appear in the magazines first. He was the most professional member of the group too. He didn't do drugs. He had a steady girlfriend. There were even a few people in suits and ties who thought *he* should be the face of the band, not John or Paul.

His name was Pete Best. And in 1962, after landing their first record contract, the other three members of the Beatles quietly got together and asked their manager, Brian Epstein, to fire him. Epstein agonized over the decision. He liked Pete, so he put it off, hoping the other three guys would change their minds.

Months later, a mere three days before the recording of the first record began, Epstein finally called Best to his office. There, the manager unceremoniously told him to piss off and find another band. He gave no reason, no explanation, no condolences—just told him that the other guys wanted him out of the group, so, uh, best of luck.

As a replacement, the band brought in some oddball named Ringo Starr. Ringo was older and had a big, funny nose. Ringo agreed to get the same ugly haircut as John, Paul, and George, and insisted on writing songs about octopuses and submarines. The other guys said, Sure, fuck it, why not?

Within six months of Best's firing, Beatlemania had erupted, making John, Paul, George, and ~~Pete~~ Ringo arguably four of the most famous faces on the entire planet.

Meanwhile, Best understandably fell into a deep depression and spent a lot of time doing what any Englishman will do if you give him a reason to: drink.

The rest of the sixties were not kind to Pete Best. By 1965, he had sued two of the Beatles for slander, and all of his other musical projects had failed horribly. In 1968, he attempted suicide, only to be talked out of it by his mother. His life was a wreck.

Best didn't have the same redemptive story Dave Mustaine did. He never became a global superstar or made millions of dollars. Yet, in many ways, Best ended up better off than Mustaine. In an interview in 1994, Best said, "I'm happier than I would have been with the Beatles."

What the hell?

Best explained that the circumstances of his getting kicked out of the Beatles ultimately led him to meet his wife. And then his marriage led him to having children. His values changed. He began to measure his life differently. Fame and glory would have been nice, sure—but he decided that what he already had was more important: a big and loving family, a stable marriage, a simple life. He even still got to play drums, touring Europe and recording albums well into the 2000s. So what was really lost? Just a lot of attention and adulation, whereas what was gained meant so much more to him.

These stories suggest that some values and metrics are better than others. Some lead to good problems that are easily and regularly solved. Others lead to bad problems that are not easily and regularly solved.

Shitty Values

There are a handful of common values that create really poor problems for people—problems that can hardly be solved. So let's go over some of them quickly:

1. *Pleasure.* Pleasure is great, but it's a horrible value to prioritize your life around. Ask any drug addict how his pursuit of pleasure turned out. Ask an adulterer who shattered her family and lost her children whether pleasure ultimately made her happy. Ask a man who almost ate himself to death how pleasure helped him solve his problems.

   Pleasure is a false god. Research shows that people who focus their energy on superficial pleasures end up more anxious, more emotionally unstable, and more depressed. Pleasure is the most superficial form of life satisfaction and therefore the easiest to obtain and the easiest to lose.

   And yet, pleasure is what's marketed to us, twenty-four/seven. It's what we fixate on. It's what we use to numb and distract ourselves. But pleasure, while necessary in life (in certain doses), isn't, by itself, sufficient.

   Pleasure is not the cause of happiness; rather, it is the effect. If you get the other stuff right (the other values and metrics), then pleasure will naturally occur as a by-product.

2. *Material Success.* Many people measure their self-worth based on how much money they make or what kind of car they drive or whether their front lawn is greener and prettier than the next-door neighbor's.

   Research shows that once one is able to provide for basic physical needs (food, shelter, and so on), the correlation between happiness and worldly success quickly approaches zero. So if you're starving and living on the street in the middle of India, an extra ten thousand dollars a year would affect your happiness a lot. But if you're sitting pretty in the middle class in a developed country, an extra ten thousand dollars per year won't affect anything much—meaning that you're killing yourself working overtime and weekends for basically nothing.

The other issue with overvaluing material success is the danger of prioritizing it over other values, such as honesty, nonviolence, and compassion. When people measure themselves not by their behavior, but by the status symbols they're able to collect, then not only are they shallow, but they're probably assholes as well.

3. *Always Being Right.* Our brains are inefficient machines. We consistently make poor assumptions, misjudge probabilities, misremember facts, give in to cognitive biases, and make decisions based on our emotional whims. As humans, we're wrong pretty much constantly, so if your metric for life success is to be right—well, you're going to have a difficult time rationalizing all of the bullshit to yourself.

The fact is, people who base their self-worth on being right about everything prevent themselves from learning from their mistakes. They lack the ability to take on new perspectives and empathize with others. They close themselves off to new and important information.

It's far more helpful to assume that you're ignorant and don't know a whole lot. This keeps you unattached to superstitious or poorly informed beliefs and promotes a constant state of learning and growth.

4. *Staying Positive.* Then there are those who measure their lives by the ability to be positive about, well, pretty much everything. Lost your job? Great! That's an opportunity to explore your passions. Husband cheated on you with your sister? Well, at least you're learning what you really mean to the people around you. Child dying of throat cancer? At least you don't have to pay for college anymore!

While there is something to be said for "staying on the sunny side of life," the truth is, sometimes life sucks, and the healthiest thing you can do is admit it.

Denying negative emotions leads to experiencing deeper and more prolonged negative emotions and to emotional dysfunction. Constant positivity is a form of avoidance, not a valid solution to life's problems—problems which, by the way, if you're choosing the right values and metrics, should be invigorating you and motivating you.

It's simple, really: things go wrong, people upset us, accidents happen. These things make us feel like shit. And that's fine. Negative emotions are a necessary component of emotional health. To deny that negativity is to *perpetuate* problems rather than solve them.

The trick with negative emotions is to 1) express them in a socially acceptable and healthy manner and 2) express them in a way that aligns with your values. Simple example: A value of mine is nonviolence. Therefore, when I get mad at somebody, I express that anger, but I also make a point of not punching them in the face. Radical idea, I know. But the anger is not the problem.

Anger is natural. Anger is a part of life. Anger is arguably quite healthy in many situations. (Remember, emotions are just feedback.)

See, it's the punching people in the face that's the problem. Not the anger. The anger is merely the messenger for my fist in your face. Don't blame the messenger. Blame my fist (or your face).

When we force ourselves to stay positive at all times, we deny the existence of our life's problems. And when we deny our problems, we rob ourselves of the chance to solve them and generate happiness. Problems add a sense of meaning and importance to our life. Thus to duck our problems is to lead a meaningless (even if supposedly pleasant) existence.

In the long run, completing a marathon makes us happier than eating a chocolate cake. Raising a child makes us happier than beating a video game. Starting a small business with friends while struggling to make ends meet makes us happier than buying a new computer. These activities are stressful, arduous, and often unpleasant. They also require withstanding problem after problem. Yet they are some of the most meaningful moments and joyous things we'll ever do. They involve pain, struggle, even anger and despair—yet once they're accomplished, we look back and get all misty-eyed telling our grandkids about them.

As Freud once said, "One day, in retrospect, the years of struggle will strike you as the most beautiful."

This is why these values—pleasure, material success, always being right, staying positive—are poor ideals for a person's life. Some of the greatest moments of one's life are *not* pleasant, *not* successful, *not* known, and *not* positive.

The point is to nail down some good values and metrics, and pleasure and success will naturally emerge as a result. These things are side effects of good values. By themselves, they are empty highs.

Defining Good and Bad Values

Good values are 1) reality-based, 2) socially constructive, and 3) immediate and controllable.

Bad values are 1) superstitious, 2) socially destructive, and 3) not immediate or controllable.

Honesty is a good value because it's something you have complete control over, it reflects reality, and it benefits others (even if it's sometimes unpleasant). Popularity, on the other hand, is a bad value. If that's your value, and if your metric is being the most popular guy/girl at the dance party, much of what happens will be out of your control: you don't know who else will be at the event, and you probably won't know who half those people are. Second, the value/metric isn't based on reality: you may *feel* popular or unpopular, when in fact you have no fucking clue what anybody else really thinks about you. (Side Note: As a rule, people who are terrified of what others think about them are actually terrified of all the shitty things they think about themselves being reflected back at them.)

Some examples of good, healthy values: honesty,

innovation, vulnerability, standing up for oneself, standing up for others, self-respect, curiosity, charity, humility,
creativity.

Some examples of bad, unhealthy values: dominance
through manipulation or violence, indiscriminate fucking,
feeling good all the time, always being the center of attention, not being alone, being liked by everybody, being rich
for the sake of being rich, sacrificing small animals to the
pagan gods.

You'll notice that good, healthy values are achieved in-
ternally. Something like creativity or humility can be experienced right now. You simply have to orient your mind
in a certain way to experience it. These values are immediate and controllable and engage you with the world as it is
rather than how you wish it were.

Bad values are generally reliant on external events—
flying in a private jet, being told you're right all the time,
owning a house in the Bahamas, eating a cannoli while getting blown by three strippers. Bad values, while sometimes
fun or pleasurable, lie outside of your control and often require socially destructive or superstitious means to achieve.

Values are about prioritization. *Everybody* would love
a good cannoli or a house in the Bahamas. The question
is your priorities. What are the values that you prioritize
above everything else, and that therefore influence your
decision-making more than anything else?

Hiroo Onoda's highest value was complete loyalty and
service to the Japanese empire. This value, in case you
couldn't tell from reading about him, stank worse than

a rotten sushi roll. It created really shitty problems for Hiroo—namely, he got stuck on a remote island where he lived off bugs and worms for thirty years. Oh, and he felt compelled to murder innocent civilians too. So despite the fact that Hiroo saw himself as a success, and despite the fact he lived up to his metrics, I think we can all agree that his life really sucked—none of us would trade shoes with him given the opportunity, nor would we commend his actions.

Dave Mustaine achieved great fame and glory and felt like a failure anyway. This is because he'd adopted a crappy value based on some arbitrary comparison to the success of others. This value gave him awful problems such as, "I need to sell 150 million more records; *then* everything will be great," and "My next tour needs to be nothing but stadiums"—problems he thought he needed to solve in order to be happy. It's no surprise that he wasn't.

On the contrary, Pete Best pulled a switcheroo. Despite being depressed and distraught by getting kicked out of the Beatles, as he grew older he learned to reprioritize what he cared about and was able to measure his life in a new light. Because of this, Best grew into a happy and healthy old man, with an easy life and great family—things that, ironically, the four Beatles would spend decades struggling to achieve or maintain.

When we have poor values—that is, poor standards we set for ourselves and others—we are essentially giving fucks about the things that don't matter, things that in fact make our life worse. But when we choose better values, we are able to divert our fucks to something better—toward things that matter, things that improve the state of our well-being and that generate happiness, pleasure, and success as side effects.

This, in a nutshell, is what "self-improvement" is really about: prioritizing better values, choosing better things to give a fuck about. Because when you give better fucks, you get better problems. And when you get better problems, you get a better life.

The rest of this book is dedicated to five counterintuitive values that I believe are the most beneficial values one can adopt. All follow the "backwards law" we talked about earlier, in that they're "negative." All require *confronting* deeper problems rather than avoiding them through highs. These five values are both unconventional and uncomfortable. But, to me, they are life-changing.

The first, which we'll look at in the next chapter, is a radical form of responsibility: taking responsibility for everything that occurs in your life, regardless of who's at fault. The second is uncertainty: the acknowledgement of your own ignorance and the cultivation of constant doubt in your own beliefs. The next is failure: the willingness to discover your own flaws and mistakes so that they may be improved upon. The fourth is rejection: the ability to both say and hear no, thus clearly defining what you will and will not accept in your life. The final value is the contemplation of one's own mortality; this one is crucial, because paying vigilant attention to one's own death is perhaps the only thing capable of helping us keep all our other values in proper perspective.

5

You Are Always Choosing

Imagine that somebody puts a gun to your head and tells you that you have to run 26.2 miles in under five hours, or else he'll kill you and your entire family.

That would suck.

Now imagine that you bought nice shoes and running gear, trained religiously for months, and completed your first marathon with all of your closest family and friends cheering you on at the finish line.

That could potentially be one of the proudest moments of your life.

Exact same 26.2 miles. Exact same person running them. Exact same pain coursing through your exact same legs. But when you chose it freely and prepared for it, it was a glorious and important milestone in your life. When it was forced upon you against your will, it was one of the most terrifying and painful experiences of your life.

Often the only difference between a problem being painful or being powerful is a sense that we *chose* it, and that we are responsible for it.

If you're miserable in your current situation, chances are it's because you feel like some part of it is outside your control—that there's a problem you have no ability to solve, a problem that was somehow thrust upon you without your choosing.

When we feel that we're choosing our problems, we feel empowered. When we feel that our problems are being forced upon us against our will, we feel victimized and miserable.

The Choice

William James had problems. Really bad problems.

Although born into a wealthy and prominent family, from birth James suffered life-threatening health issues: an eye problem that left him temporarily blinded as a child; a terrible stomach condition that caused excessive vomiting and forced him to adopt an obscure and highly sensitive diet; trouble with his hearing; back spasms so bad that for days at a time he often couldn't sit or stand upright.

Due to his health problems, James spent most of his time at home. He didn't have many friends, and he wasn't particularly good at school. Instead, he passed the days painting. That was the only thing he liked and the only thing he felt particularly good at.

Unfortunately, nobody else thought he was good at it. When he grew to adulthood, nobody bought his work. And as the years dragged on, his father (a wealthy businessman) began ridiculing him for his laziness and his lack of talent.

Meanwhile, his younger brother, Henry James, went on to become a world-renowned novelist; his sister, Alice James, made a good living as a writer as well. William was the family oddball, the black sheep.

In a desperate attempt to salvage the young man's future, James's father used his business connections to get him admitted into Harvard Medical School. It was his last chance, his father told him. If he screwed this up, there was no hope for him.

But James never felt at home or at peace at Harvard. Medicine never appealed to him. He spent the whole time feeling like a fake and a fraud. After all, if he couldn't overcome his own problems, how could he ever hope to have the energy to help others with theirs? After touring a psychiatric facility one day, James mused in his diary that he felt he had more in common with the patients than with the doctors.

A few years went by and, again to his father's disapproval, James dropped out of medical school. But rather than deal with the brunt of his father's wrath, he decided to get away: he signed up to join an anthropological expedition to the Amazon rain forest.

This was in the 1860s, so transcontinental travel was difficult and dangerous. If you ever played the computer game *Oregon Trail* when you were a kid, it was kind of like that, with the dysentery and drowning oxen and everything.

Anyway, James made it all the way to the Amazon, where the real adventure was to begin. Surprisingly, his fragile health held up that whole way. But once he finally made it, on the first day of the expedition, he promptly contracted smallpox and nearly died in the jungle.

Then his back spasms returned, painful to the point of making James unable to walk. By this time, he was emaciated and starved from the smallpox, immobilized by his bad back, and left alone in the middle of South America (the rest of the expedition having gone on without him) with no clear way to get home—a journey that would take months and likely kill him anyway.

But somehow he eventually made it back to New England, where he was greeted by an (even more) disappointed father. By this point the young man wasn't so young anymore—nearly thirty years old, still unemployed, a failure at everything he had attempted, with a body that routinely betrayed him and wasn't likely to ever get better. Despite all the advantages and opportunities he'd been given in life, everything had fallen apart. The only constants in his life seemed to be suffering and disappointment. James fell into a deep depression and began making plans to take his own life.

But one night, while reading lectures by the philosopher Charles Peirce, James decided to conduct a little experiment. In his diary, he wrote that he would spend one year believing that he was 100 percent responsible for everything that occurred in his life, no matter what. During this period, he would do everything in his power to change his circumstances, no matter the likelihood of failure. If nothing improved in that year, then it would be apparent that he was truly powerless to the circumstances around him, and then he would take his own life.

The punch line? William James went on to become the father of American psychology. His work has been translated into a bazillion languages, and he's regarded as one of the most influential intellectuals/philosophers/psychologists of his generation. He would go on to teach at Harvard and would tour much of the United States and Europe giving lectures. He would marry and have five children (one of whom, Henry, would become a famous biographer and win a Pulitzer Prize). James would later refer to his little experiment as his "rebirth," and would credit it with *everything* that he later accomplished in his life.

There is a simple realization from which all personal improvement and growth emerges. This is the realization that we, individually, are responsible for everything in our lives, no matter the external circumstances.

We don't always control what happens to us. But we *always* control how we interpret what happens to us, as well as how we respond.

Whether we consciously recognize it or not, we are always responsible for our experiences. It's impossible not to be. Choosing to *not* consciously interpret events in our lives is still an interpretation of the events of our lives. Choosing to *not* respond to the events in our lives is still a response to the events in our lives. Even if you get run over by a clown car and pissed on by a busload of schoolchildren, it's still *your responsibility* to interpret the meaning of the event and choose a response.

Whether we like it or not, we are *always* taking an active role in what's occurring to and within us. We are always interpreting the meaning of every moment and every occurrence. We are always choosing the values by which we live and the metrics by which we measure everything that happens to us. Often the same event can be good or bad, depending on the metric we choose to use.

The point is, we are *always* choosing, whether we recognize it or not. Always.

It comes back to how, in reality, there is no such thing as not giving a single fuck. It's impossible. We must all give a fuck about something. To not give a fuck about *anything* is still to give a fuck about *something*.

The real question is, What are we choosing to give a fuck about? What values are we choosing to base our actions on? What metrics are we choosing to use to measure our life? And are those *good* choices—good values and good metrics?

The Responsibility/Fault Fallacy

Years ago, when I was much younger and stupider, I wrote a blog post, and at the end of it I said something like, "And as a great philosopher once said: 'With great power comes great responsibility.'" It sounded nice and authoritative. I couldn't remember who had said it, and my Google search had turned up nothing, but I stuck it in there anyway. It fit the post nicely.

About ten minutes later, the first comment came in: "I think the 'great philosopher' you're referring to is Uncle Ben from the movie *Spider-Man*."

As another great philosopher once said, "Doh!"

"With great power comes great responsibility." The last words of Uncle Ben before a thief whom Peter Parker let get away murders him on a sidewalk full of people for absolutely no explicable reason. *That* great philosopher.

Still, we've all heard the quote. It gets repeated a lot—usually ironically and after about seven beers. It's one of those perfect quotes that sound really intelligent, and yet it's basically just telling you what you already know, even if you've never quite thought about the matter before.

"With great power comes great responsibility."

It is true. But there's a better version of this quote, a version that actually *is* profound, and all you have to do is switch the nouns around: "With great responsibility comes great power."

The more we choose to accept responsibility in our lives, the more power we will exercise over our lives. Accepting responsibility for our problems is thus the first step to solving them.

I once knew a man who was convinced that the reason no woman would date him was because he was too short. He was educated, interesting, and good-looking—a good catch, in principle—but he was absolutely convinced that women found him too short to date.

And because *he* felt that he was too short, he didn't often go out and try to meet women. The few times he did, he would hone in on the smallest behaviors from any woman he talked with that could possibly indicate he wasn't attractive enough for her and then convince himself that she didn't like him, even if she really did. As you can imagine, his dating life sucked.

What he didn't realize was that *he* had chosen the value that was hurting him: height. Women, he assumed, are attracted only to height. He was screwed, no matter what he did.

This choice of value was disempowering. It gave this man a really crappy problem: not being tall enough in a world meant (in his view) for tall people. There are far better values that he could have adopted in his dating life. "I want to date only women who like me for who I am" might have been a nice place to start—a metric that assesses the values of honesty and acceptance. But he did not choose these values. He likely wasn't even aware that he *was* choosing his value (or *could* do so). Even though he didn't realize it, he was responsible for his own problems.

Despite that responsibility, he went on complaining: "But I don't have a choice," he would tell the bartender. "There's nothing I can do! Women are superficial and vain and will never like me!" Yes, it's *every single woman's fault* for not liking a self-pitying, shallow guy with shitty values. Obviously.

A lot of people hesitate to take responsibility for their problems because they believe that to be *responsible* for your problems is to also be *at fault* for your problems.

Responsibility and fault often appear together in our

culture. But they're not the same thing. If I hit you with my car, I am both at fault and likely legally responsible to compensate you in some way. Even if hitting you with my car was an accident, I am still responsible. This is the way fault works in our society: if you fuck up, you're on the hook for making it right. And it should be that way.

But there are also problems that we *aren't* at fault for, yet we are still responsible for them.

For example, if you woke up one day and there was a newborn baby on your doorstep, it would not be your *fault* that the baby had been put there, but the baby would now be your *responsibility*. You would have to choose what to do. And whatever you ended up choosing (keeping it, getting rid of it, ignoring it, feeding it to a pit bull), there would be problems associated with your choice—and you would be responsible for those as well.

Judges don't get to choose their cases. When a case goes to court, the judge assigned to it did not commit the crime, was not a witness to the crime, and was not affected by the crime, but he or she is still *responsible* for the crime. The judge must then choose the consequences; he or she must identify the metric against which the crime will be measured and make sure that the chosen metric is carried out.

We are responsible for experiences that aren't our fault all the time. This is part of life.

Here's one way to think about the distinction between the two concepts. Fault is past tense. Responsibility is present tense. Fault results from choices that have already been made. Responsibility results from the choices you're currently making, every second of every day. You are choosing to read this. You are choosing to think about the concepts. You are choosing to accept or reject the concepts. It may be *my* fault that you think my ideas are lame, but *you* are responsible for coming to your own conclusions. It's not *your* fault that I chose to write this sentence, but you are still responsible for choosing to read it (or not).

There's a difference between blaming someone else for your situation and that person's actually being responsible for your situation. Nobody else is ever responsible for your situation but you. Many people may be to blame for your unhappiness, but nobody is ever *responsible* for your unhappiness but you. This is because *you* always get to choose how you see things, how you react to things, how you value things. You always get to choose the metric by which to measure your experiences.

My first girlfriend dumped me in spectacular fashion. She was cheating on me with her teacher. It was awesome. And by awesome, I mean it felt like getting punched in the stomach about 253 times. To make things worse, when I confronted her about it, she promptly left me for him. Three years together, down the toilet just like that.

I was miserable for months afterward. That was to be expected. But I also held her responsible for my misery. Which, take it from me, didn't get me very far. It just made the misery worse.

See, I couldn't control her. No matter how many times I called her, or screamed at her, or begged her to take me back, or made surprise visits to her place, or did other creepy and irrational ex-boyfriend things, I could never control her emotions or her actions. Ultimately, while she was *to blame* for how I felt, she was never *responsible* for how I felt. I was.

At some point, after enough tears and alcohol, my thinking began to shift and I began to understand that although she had done something horrible to me and she could be blamed for that, it was now my own responsibility to make myself happy again. She was never going to pop up and fix things for me. I had to fix them for myself.

When I took that approach, a few things happened. First, I began to improve myself. I started exercising and spending more time with my friends (whom I had been neglecting). I started deliberately meeting new people. I took a big study-abroad trip and did some volunteer work. And slowly, I started to feel better.

I still resented my ex for what she had done. But at least now I was taking responsibility for my own emotions. And by doing so, I was choosing better values—values aimed at taking care of myself, learning to feel better about myself, rather than aimed at getting her to fix what she'd broken.

(By the way, this whole "holding her responsible for my emotions" thing is probably part of why she left in the first place. More on that in a couple chapters.)

Then, about a year later, something funny began to happen. As I looked back on our relationship, I started to notice problems I had never noticed before, problems that *I* was to blame for and that *I* could have done something to solve. I realized that it was likely that I hadn't been a great boyfriend, and that people don't just magically cheat on somebody they've been with unless they are unhappy for some reason.

I'm not saying that this excused what my ex did—not at all. But recognizing my mistakes helped me to realize that I perhaps hadn't been the innocent victim I'd believed myself to be. That I had a role to play in enabling the shitty relationship to continue for as long as it did. After all, people who date each other tend to have similar values. And if I dated someone with shitty values for that long, what did that say about me and my values? I learned the hard way that if the people in your relationships are selfish and doing hurtful things, it's likely you are too, you just don't realize it.

In hindsight, I was able to look back and see warning signs of my ex-girlfriend's character, signs I had chosen to ignore or brush off when I was with her. *That* was my fault. I could look back and see that I hadn't exactly been the Boyfriend of the Year to her either. In fact, I had often been cold and arrogant toward her; other times I took her for granted and blew her off and hurt her. *These* things were my fault too.

Did my mistakes justify her mistake? No. But still, I took on the responsibility of never making those same mistakes again, and never overlooking the same signs again, to help guarantee that I will never suffer the same consequences again. I took on the responsibility of striving to make my future relationships with women that much better. And I'm happy to report that I have. No more cheating girlfriends leaving me, no more 253 stomach punches. I took responsibility for my problems and improved upon them. I took responsibility for my role in that unhealthy relationship and improved upon it with later relationships.

And you know what? My ex leaving me, while one of the most painful experiences I've ever had, was also one of the most important and influential experiences of my life. I credit it with inspiring a significant amount of personal growth. I learned more from that single problem than dozens of my successes combined.

We all love to take responsibility for success and happiness. Hell, we often *fight over* who gets to be responsible for success and happiness. But taking responsibility for our problems is far more important, because that's where the real learning comes from. That's where the real-life improvement comes from. To simply blame others is only to hurt yourself.

Responding to Tragedy

But what about really awful events? A lot of people can get on board with taking responsibility for work-related problems and maybe watching too much TV when they should really be playing with their kids or being productive. But when it comes to horrible tragedies, they pull the emergency cord on the responsibility train and get off when it stops. Some things just feel too painful for them to own up to.

But think about it: the intensity of the event doesn't change the underlying truth. If you get robbed, say, you're obviously not at fault for being robbed. No one would ever choose to go through that. But as with the baby on your doorstep, you are immediately thrust into responsibility for a life-and-death situation. Do you fight back? Do you panic? Do you freeze up? Do you tell the police? Do you try to forget it and pretend it never happened? These are all choices and reactions you're responsible for making or rejecting. You didn't choose the robbery, but it's still your responsibility to manage the emotional and psychological (and legal) fallout of the experience.

In 2008, the Taliban took control of the Swat Valley, a remote part of northeastern Pakistan. They quickly implemented their Muslim extremist agenda. No television. No films. No women outside the house without a male escort. No girls attending school.

By 2009, an eleven-year-old Pakistani girl named Malala Yousafzai had begun to speak out against the school ban. She continued to attend her local school, risking both her and her father's lives; she also attended conferences in nearby cities. She wrote online, "How dare the Taliban take away my right for education?"

In 2012, at the age of fourteen, she was shot in the face as she rode the bus home from school one day. A masked Taliban soldier armed with a rifle boarded the bus and asked, "Who is Malala? Tell me, or I will shoot everyone here." Malala identified herself (an amazing choice in and of itself), and the man shot her in the head in front of all the other passengers.

Malala went into a coma and almost died. The Taliban

stated publicly that if she somehow survived the attempt, they would kill both her and her father.

Today, Malala is still alive. She still speaks out against violence and oppression toward women in Muslim countries, now as a best-selling author. In 2014 she received the Nobel Peace Prize for her efforts. It would seem that being shot in the face only gave her a larger audience and more courage than before. It would have been easy for her to lie down and say, "I can't do anything," or "I have no choice." That, ironically, would still have been her choice. But she chose the opposite.

A few years ago, I had written about some of the ideas in this chapter on my blog, and a man left a comment. He said that I was shallow and superficial, adding that I had no real understanding of life's problems or human responsibility. He said that his son had recently died in a car accident. He accused me of not knowing what true pain was and said that I was an asshole for suggesting that he himself was responsible for the pain he felt over his son's death.

This man had obviously suffered pain much greater than most people ever have to confront in their lives. He didn't choose for his son to die, nor was it his fault that his son died. The responsibility for coping with that loss was given to him even though it was clearly and understandably unwanted. But despite all that, he was still responsible for his own emotions, beliefs, and actions. How he reacted to his son's death was his own choice. Pain of one sort or another is inevitable for all of us, but we get to choose what it means to and for us. Even in claiming that he had *no* choice in the matter and simply wanted his son back, he was making a choice—one of many ways he could have chosen to use that pain.

Of course, I didn't say any of this to him. I was too busy being horrified and thinking that yes, perhaps I was way in over my head and had no idea what the fuck I was talking about. That's a hazard that comes with my line of work. A problem that I chose. And a problem that I was responsible for dealing with.

At first, I felt awful. But then, after a few minutes, I began to get angry. His objections had little to do with what I was actually saying, I told myself. And what the hell? Just because I don't have a kid who died doesn't mean I haven't experienced terrible pain myself.

But then I actually applied my own advice. I chose my problem. I could get mad at this man and argue with him, try to "outpain" him with my own pain, which would just make us both look stupid and insensitive. Or I could choose a better problem, working on practicing patience, understanding my readers better, and keeping that man in mind every time I wrote about pain and trauma from then on. And that's what I've tried to do.

I replied simply that I was sorry for his loss and left it at that. What else can you say?

Genetics and the Hand We're Dealt

In 2013, the BBC rounded up half a dozen teenagers with obsessive-compulsive disorder (OCD) and followed them as they attended intensive therapies to help them overcome their unwanted thoughts and repetitive behaviors.

There was Imogen, a seventeen-year-old girl who had a compulsive need to tap every surface she walked past; if she failed to do so, she was flooded with horrible thoughts of her family dying. There was Josh, who needed to do everything with both sides of his body—shake a person's hand with both his right and his left hand, eat his food with each hand, step through a doorway with both feet, and so on. If he didn't "equalize" his two sides, he suffered from severe panic attacks. And then there was Jack, a classic germophobe who refused to leave his house without wearing gloves, boiled all his water before drinking it, and refused to eat food not cleaned and prepared himself.

OCD is a terrible neurological and genetic disorder that cannot be cured. At best, it can be managed. And, as we'll see, managing the disorder comes down to managing one's values.

The first thing the psychiatrists on this project do is tell the kids that they're to accept the imperfections of their compulsive desires. What that means, as one example, is that when Imogen becomes flooded with horrible thoughts of her family dying, she is to accept that her family may actually die and that there's nothing she can do about it; simply put, she is told that what happens to her is not her fault. Josh is forced to accept that over the long term, "equalizing" all of his behaviors to make them symmetrical is actually destroying his life more than occasional panic attacks would. And Jack is reminded that no matter what he does, germs are always present and always infecting him.

The goal is to get the kids to recognize that their values are not rational—that in fact their values are not even theirs, but rather are the disorder's—and that by fulfilling these irrational values they are actually harming their ability to function in life.

The next step is to encourage the kids to choose a value that is more important than their OCD value and to focus on that. For Josh, it's the possibility of not having to hide his disorder from his friends and family all the time, the prospect of having a normal, functioning social life. For Imogen, it's the idea of taking control over her own thoughts and feelings and being happy again. And for Jack, it's the ability to leave his house for long periods of time without suffering traumatic episodes.

With these new values held front and center in their minds, the teenagers set out on intensive desensitization exercises that force them to live out their new values. Panic attacks ensue; tears are shed; Jack punches an array of inanimate objects and then immediately washes his hands. But by the end of the documentary, major progress has been made. Imogen no longer needs to tap every surface she comes across. She says, "There are still monsters in the back of my mind, and there probably always will be, but they're getting quieter now." Josh is able to go periods of twenty-five to thirty minutes without "equalizing" his behaviors between both sides of his body. And Jack, who makes perhaps the most improvement, is actually able to go out to restaurants and drink out of bottles and glasses without washing them first. Jack sums up well what he learned: "I didn't choose this life; I didn't choose this horrible, horrible condition. But I get to choose how to live with it; I *have to* choose how to live with it."

A lot of people treat being born with a disadvantage, whether OCD or small stature or something very different, as though they were screwed out of something highly valuable. They feel that there's nothing they can do about it, so they avoid responsibility for their situation. They figure, "I didn't choose my crappy genetics, so it's not my fault if things go wrong."

And it's true, it's not their fault.

But it's still their responsibility.

Back in college, I had a bit of a delusional fantasy of becoming a professional poker player. I won money and everything, and it was fun, but after almost a year of serious play, I quit. The lifestyle of staying up all night staring at a computer screen, winning thousands of dollars one day and then losing most of it the next, wasn't for me, and it wasn't exactly the most healthy or emotionally stable means of earning a living. But my time playing poker had a surprisingly profound influence on the way I see life.

The beauty of poker is that while luck is always involved, luck doesn't dictate the long-term results of the game. A person can get dealt terrible cards and beat someone who was dealt great cards. Sure, the person who gets dealt great cards has a higher likelihood of winning the hand, but ultimately the winner is determined by—yup, you guessed it—the *choices* each player makes through-out play.

I see life in the same terms. We all get dealt cards. Some of us get better cards than others. And while it's easy to get hung up on our cards, and feel we got screwed over, the real game lies in the choices we make with those cards, the risks we decide to take, and the consequences we choose to live with. People who consistently make the best choices in the situations they're given are the ones who eventually come out ahead in poker, just as in life. And it's not necessarily the people with the best cards.

There are those who suffer psychologically and emotion-ally from neurological and/or genetic deficiencies. But this changes nothing. Sure, they inherited a bad hand and are not to blame. No more than the short guy wanting to get a date is to blame for being short. Or the person who got robbed is to blame for being robbed. But it's still their responsibility. Whether they choose to seek psychiatric treatment, under-go therapy, or do nothing, the choice is ultimately theirs to make. There are those who suffer through bad childhoods. There are those who are abused and violated and screwed over, physically, emotionally, financially. They are not to blame for their problems and their hindrances, but they are still responsible—*always* responsible—to move on despite their problems and to make the best choices they can, given their circumstances.

And let's be honest here. If you were to add up *all* of the people who have some psychiatric disorder, struggle with depression or suicidal thoughts, have been subjected to neglect or abuse, have dealt with tragedy or the death of a loved one, and have survived serious health issues, accidents, or trauma—if you were to round up *all of those people* and put them in the room, well, you'd probably have to round up everyone, because nobody makes it through life without collecting a few scars on the way out.

Sure, some people get saddled with worse problems than others. And some people are legitimately victimized in horrible ways. But as much as this may upset us or disturb us, it ultimately changes nothing about the responsibility equation of our individual situation.

Victimhood Chic

The responsibility/fault fallacy allows people to pass off the responsibility for solving their problems to others. This ability to alleviate responsibility through blame gives people a temporary high and a feeling of moral righteousness.

Unfortunately, one side effect of the Internet and social media is that it's become easier than ever to push responsibility—for even the tiniest of infractions—onto some other group or person. In fact, this kind of public blame/shame game has become popular; in certain crowds it's even seen as "cool." The public sharing of "injustices" garners far more attention and emotional outpouring than most other events on social media, rewarding people who are able to perpetually feel victimized with ever-growing amounts of attention and sympathy.

"Victimhood chic" is in style on both the right and the left today, among both the rich and the poor. In fact, this may be the first time in human history that every single demographic group has felt unfairly victimized simultaneously. And they're all riding the highs of the moral indignation that comes along with it.

Right now, *anyone* who is offended about *anything*—whether it's the fact that a book about racism was assigned in a university class, or that Christmas trees were banned at the local mall, or the fact that taxes were raised half a percent on investment funds—feels as though they're being oppressed in some way and therefore deserve to be outraged and to have a certain amount of attention.

The current media environment both encourages and perpetuates these reactions because, after all, it's good for business. The writer and media commentator Ryan Holiday refers to this as "outrage porn": rather than report on real stories and real issues, the media find it much easier (and more profitable) to find something mildly offensive, broadcast it to a wide audience, generate outrage, and then broadcast that outrage back across the population in a way that outrages yet another part of the population. This triggers a kind of echo of bullshit pinging back and forth between two imaginary sides, meanwhile distracting everyone from real societal problems. It's no wonder we're more politically polarized than ever before.

The biggest problem with victimhood chic is that it sucks attention away from *actual* victims. It's like the boy who cried wolf. The more people there are who proclaim themselves victims over tiny infractions, the harder it becomes to see who the real victims actually are.

People get addicted to feeling offended all the time because it gives them a high; being self-righteous and morally superior feels *good*. As political cartoonist Tim Kreider put it in a *New York Times* op-ed: "Outrage is like a lot of other things that feel good but over time devour us from the inside out. And it's even more insidious than most vices because we don't even consciously acknowledge that it's a pleasure."

But part of living in a democracy and a free society is that we all have to deal with views and people we don't necessarily like. That's simply the price we pay—you could even say it's the whole point of the system. And it seems more and more people are forgetting that.

We should pick our battles carefully, while simultaneously attempting to empathize a bit with the so-called enemy. We should approach the news and media with a healthy dose of skepticism and avoid painting those who disagree with us with a broad brush. We should prioritize values of being honest, fostering transparency, and welcoming doubt over the values of being right, feeling good, and getting revenge. These "democratic" values are harder to maintain amidst the constant noise of a networked world. But we must accept the responsibility and nurture them regardless. The future stability of our political systems may depend on it.

There Is No "How"

A lot of people might hear all of this and then say something like, "Okay, but how? I get that my values suck and that I avoid responsibility for all of my problems and that I'm an entitled little shit who thinks the world should revolve around me and every inconvenience I experience—but *how* do I change?"

And to this I say, in my best Yoda impersonation: "Do, or do not; there is no 'how.'"

You are *already choosing,* in every moment of every day, what to give a fuck about, so change is as simple as choosing to give a fuck about something else.

It really *is* that simple. It's just not easy.

It's not easy because you're going to feel like a loser, a fraud, a dumbass at first. You're going to be nervous. You're going to freak out. You may get pissed off at your wife or your friends or your father in the process. These are all side effects of changing your values, of changing the fucks you're giving. But they are inevitable.

It's simple but really, really hard.

Let's look at some of these side effects. You're going to feel uncertain; I guarantee it. "Should I really give this up? Is this the right thing to do?" Giving up a value you've depended on for years is going to feel disorienting, as if you don't really know right from wrong anymore. This is hard, but it's normal.

Next, you'll feel like a failure. You've spent half your life measuring yourself by that old value, so when you change your priorities, change your metrics, and stop behaving in the same way, you'll fail to meet that old, trusted metric and thus immediately feel like some sort of fraud or nobody. This is also normal and also uncomfortable.

And certainly you will weather rejections. Many of the relationships in your life were built around the values you've been keeping, so the moment you change those values—the moment you decide that studying is more important than partying, that getting married and having a family is more important than rampant sex, that working a job you believe in is more important than money—your turnaround will reverberate out through your relationships, and many of them will blow up in your face. This too is normal and this too will be uncomfortable.

These are necessary, though painful, side effects of choosing to place your fucks elsewhere, in a place far more important and more worthy of your energies. As you reassess your values, you will be met with internal and external resistance along the way. More than anything, you will feel uncertain; you will wonder if what you're doing is wrong.

But as we'll see, this is a good thing.

6

You're Wrong About Everything (But So Am I)

Five hundred years ago cartographers believed that California was an island. Doctors believed that slicing a person's arm open (or causing bleeding anywhere) could cure disease. Scientists believed that fire was made out of something called phlogiston. Women believed that rubbing dog urine on their face had anti-aging benefits. Astronomers believed that the sun revolved around the earth.

When I was a little boy, I used to think "mediocre" was a kind of vegetable that I didn't want to eat. I thought my brother had found a secret passageway in my grandmother's house because he could get outside without having to leave the bathroom (spoiler alert: there was a window). I also thought that when my friend and his family visited

"Washington, B.C.," they had somehow traveled back in time to when the dinosaurs lived, because after all, "B.C." was a long time ago.

As a teenager, I told everybody that I didn't care about anything, when the truth was I cared about way too much. Other people ruled my world without my even knowing. I thought happiness was a destiny and not a choice. I thought love was something that just happened, not something that you worked for. I thought being "cool" had to be practiced and learned from others, rather than invented for oneself.

When I was with my first girlfriend, I thought we would be together forever. And then, when that relationship ended, I thought I'd never feel the same way about a woman again. And then when I felt the same way about a woman again, I thought that love sometimes just wasn't enough. And then I realized that each individual gets to *decide* what is "enough," and that love can be whatever we let it be.

Every step of the way I was wrong. About everything. Throughout my life, I've been flat-out wrong about myself, others, society, culture, the world, the universe—everything.

And I hope that will continue to be the case for the rest of my life.

Just as Present Mark can look back on Past Mark's every flaw and mistake, one day Future Mark will look back on Present Mark's assumptions (including the contents of this book) and notice similar flaws. And that will be a good thing. Because that will mean I have grown.

There's a famous Michael Jordan quote about him failing over and over and over again, and that's why he succeeded.

Well, I'm always wrong about everything, over and over and over again, and that's why my life improves.

Growth is an endlessly *iterative* process. When we learn something new, we don't go from "wrong" to "right." Rather, we go from wrong to slightly less wrong. And when we learn something additional, we go from slightly less wrong to slightly less wrong than that, and then to even less wrong than that, and so on. We are always in the process of approaching truth and perfection without actually ever reaching truth or perfection.

We shouldn't seek to find the ultimate "right" answer for ourselves, but rather, we should seek to chip away at the ways that we're wrong today so that we can be a little less wrong tomorrow.

When viewed from this perspective, personal growth can actually be quite scientific. Our values are our hypotheses: this behavior is good and important; that other behavior is not. Our actions are the experiments; the resulting emotions and thought patterns are our data.

There is no correct dogma or perfect ideology. There is only what your experience has shown you to be right *for you*—and even then, that experience is probably somewhat wrong too. And because you and I and everybody else all have differing needs and personal histories and life circumstances, we will all inevitably come to differing "correct" answers about what our lives mean and how they should be lived. My correct answer involves traveling alone for years on end, living in obscure places, and laughing at my own farts. Or at least that was the correct answer up until recently. That answer will change and evolve, because I change and evolve; and as I grow older and more experienced, I chip away at how wrong I am, becoming less and less wrong every day.

Many people become so obsessed with being "right" about their life that they never end up actually *living* it.

A certain woman is single and lonely and wants a partner, but she never gets out of the house and does anything about it. A certain man works his ass off and believes he deserves a promotion, but he never explicitly says that to his boss.

They're told that they're afraid of failure, of rejection, of someone saying no.

But that's not it. Sure, rejection hurts. Failure sucks. But there are particular certainties that we hold on to—certainties that we're afraid to question or let go of, values that have given our lives meaning over the years. That woman doesn't get out there and date because she would be forced to confront her beliefs about her own desirability. That man doesn't ask for the promotion because he would have to confront his beliefs about what his skills are actually worth.

It's easier to sit in a painful certainty that nobody would find you attractive, that nobody appreciates your talents, than to actually *test* those beliefs and find out for sure.

Beliefs of this sort—that I'm not attractive enough, so why bother; or that my boss is an asshole, so why bother—are designed to give us moderate comfort now by mortgaging greater happiness and success later on. They're terrible long-term strategies, yet we cling to them because we assume we're right, because we assume we already know what's supposed to happen. In other words, we assume we know how the story ends.

Certainty is the enemy of growth. Nothing is for certain until it has already happened—and even then, it's still debatable. That's why accepting the inevitable imperfections of our values is necessary for any growth to take place.

Instead of striving for certainty, we should be in constant search of doubt: doubt about our own beliefs, doubt about our own feelings, doubt about what the future may hold for us unless we get out there and create it for ourselves. Instead of looking to be right all the time, we should be looking for how we're wrong all the time. Because we are.

Being wrong opens us up to the possibility of change. Being wrong brings the opportunity for growth. It means not cutting your arm open to cure a cold or splashing dog piss on your face to look young again. It means not thinking "mediocre" is a vegetable, and not being afraid to care about things.

Because here's something that's weird but true: we don't *actually* know what a positive or negative experience is. Some of the most difficult and stressful moments of our lives also end up being the most formative and motivating. Some of the best and most gratifying experiences of our lives are also the most distracting and demotivating. Don't trust your conception of positive/negative experiences. All that we know for certain is what hurts in the moment and what doesn't. And that's not worth much.

Just as we look back in horror at the lives of people five hundred years ago, I imagine people five hundred years from now will laugh at us and our certainties today. They will laugh at how we let our money and our jobs define our lives. They will laugh at how we were afraid to show appreciation for those who matter to us most, yet heaped praise on public figures who didn't deserve anything. They will laugh at our rituals and superstitions, our worries and our wars; they will gawk at our cruelty. They will study our art and argue over our history. They will understand truths about us of which none of us are yet aware.

And they, too, will be wrong. Just less wrong than we were.

Architects of Our Own Beliefs

Try this. Take a random person and put them in a room with some buttons to push. Then tell them that if they do something specific—some undefined something that they have to figure out—a light will flash on indicating that they've won a point. Then tell them to see how many points they can earn within a thirty-minute period.

When psychologists have done this, what happens is what you might expect. People sit down and start mashing buttons at random until eventually the light comes on to tell them they got a point. Logically, they then try repeating whatever they were doing to get more points. Except now the light's not coming on. So they start experimenting with more complicated sequences—press this button three times, then this button once, then wait five seconds, and—*ding!* Another point. But eventually *that* stops working. Perhaps it doesn't have to do with buttons at all, they think. Perhaps it has to do with how I'm sitting. Or what I'm touching. Maybe it has to do with my feet. *Ding!* Another point. Yeah, maybe it's my feet *and then* I press another button. *Ding!*

Generally, within ten to fifteen minutes each person has figured out the specific sequence of behaviors required to net more points. It's usually something weird like standing on one foot or memorizing a long sequence of buttons pressed in a specific amount of time while facing a certain direction.

But here's the funny part: the points really are random. There's no sequence; there's no pattern. Just a light that keeps coming on with a ding, and people doing cartwheels thinking that what they're doing is giving them points.

Sadism aside, the point of the experiment is to show how quickly the human mind is capable of coming up with and believing in a bunch of bullshit that isn't real. And it turns out, we're all really good at it. Every person leaves that room convinced that he or she nailed the experiment and won the game. They all believe that they discovered the "perfect" sequence of buttons that earned them their points. But the methods they come up with are as unique as the individuals themselves. One man came up with a long sequence of button-pushing that made no sense to anyone but himself. One girl came to believe that she had to tap the ceiling a certain number of times to get points. When she left the room she was exhausted from jumping up and down.

Our brains are meaning machines. What we understand as "meaning" is generated by the associations our brain makes between two or more experiences. We press a button, then we see a light go on; we assume the button *caused* the light to go on. This, at its core, is the basis of meaning. Button, light; light, button. We see a chair. We note that it's gray. Our brain then draws the association between the color (gray) and the object (chair) and forms meaning: "The chair is gray."

Our minds are constantly whirring, generating more and more associations to help us understand and control the environment around us. Everything about our experiences, both external and internal, generates new associations and connections within our minds. Everything from the words on this page, to the grammatical concepts you use to decipher them, to the dirty thoughts your mind wanders into when my writing becomes boring or repetitive—each of these thoughts, impulses, and perceptions is composed of thousands upon thousands of neural connections, firing in conjunction, alighting your mind in a blaze of knowledge and understanding.

But there are two problems. First, the brain is imperfect. We mistake things we see and hear. We forget things or misinterpret events quite easily.

Second, once we create meaning for ourselves, our brains are designed to hold on to that meaning. We are biased toward the meaning our mind has made, and we don't want to let go of it. Even if we see evidence that contradicts the meaning we created, we often ignore it and keep on believing anyway.

The comedian Emo Philips once said, "I used to think the human brain was the most wonderful organ in my body. Then I realized who was telling me this." The unfortunate fact is, most of what we come to "know" and believe is the product of the innate inaccuracies and biases present in our brains. Many or even most of our values are products of events that are not representative of the world at large, or are the result of a totally misconceived past.

The result of all this? Most of our beliefs are wrong. Or, to be more exact, *all* beliefs are wrong—some are just less wrong than others. The human mind is a jumble of inaccuracy. And while this may make you uncomfortable, it's an incredibly important concept to accept, as we'll see.

The Dangers of Pure Certainty

Erin sits across from me at the sushi restaurant and tries to explain why she doesn't believe in death. It's been almost three hours, and she's eaten exactly four cucumber rolls and drunk an entire bottle of sake by herself. (In fact, she's about halfway through bottle number two now.) It's four o'clock on a Tuesday afternoon.

I didn't invite her here. She found out where I was via the Internet and flew out to come find me.

Again.

She's done this before. You see, Erin is convinced that she can cure death, but she's also convinced that she needs my help to do it. But not my help in like a business sense. If she just needed some PR advice or something, that would be one thing. No, it's more than that: she needs me to be her boyfriend. Why? After three hours of questioning and a bottle and a half of sake, it still isn't clear.

My fiancée was with us in the restaurant, by the way. Erin thought it important that she be included in the discussion; Erin wanted her to know that she was "willing to share" me and that my girlfriend (now wife) "shouldn't feel threatened" by her.

I met Erin at a self-help seminar in 2008. She seemed like a nice enough person. A little bit on the woo-woo, New Agey side of things, but she was a lawyer and had gone to an Ivy League school, and was clearly smart. And she laughed at my jokes and thought I was cute—so, of course, knowing me, I slept with her.

A month later, she invited me to uproot across the country and move in with her. This struck me as somewhat of a red flag, and so I tried to break things off with her. She responded by saying that she would kill herself if I refused to be with her. Okay, so make that two red flags. I promptly blocked her from my email and all my devices.

This would slow her down but not stop her.

Years before I met her, Erin had gotten into a car accident and nearly died. Actually, she *had* medically "died" for a few moments—all brain activity had stopped—but she had somehow miraculously been revived. When she "came back," she claimed everything had changed. She became a very spiritual person. She became interested in, and started

believing in, energy healing and angels and universal consciousness and tarot cards. She also believed that she had
become a healer and an empath and that she could see
the future. And for whatever reason, upon meeting me,
she decided that she and I were destined to save the world
together. To "cure death," as she put it.

After I'd blocked her, she began to create new email ad-
dresses, sometimes sending me as many as a dozen angry
emails in a single day. She created fake Facebook and Twitter
accounts that she used to harass me as well as people close
to me. She created a website identical to mine and wrote
dozens of articles claiming that I was her ex-boyfriend and
that I had lied to her and cheated her, that I had promised
to marry her and that she and I belonged together. When I
contacted her to take the site down, she said that she would
take it down only if I flew to California to be with her. This
was her idea of a compromise.

And through all of this, her justification was the same:
I was destined to be with her, that God had preordained
it, that she literally woke up in the middle of the night to
the voices of angels commanding that "our special relationship" was to be the harbinger of a new age of permanent
peace on earth. (Yes, she really told me this.)

By the time we were sitting in that sushi restaurant together, there had been thousands of emails. Whether I responded or didn't respond, replied respectfully or replied
angrily, nothing ever changed. Her mind never changed;
her beliefs never budged. This had gone on for over seven
years by then (and counting).

And so it was, in that small sushi restaurant, with Erin guzzling sake and babbling for hours about how she'd cured her cat's kidney stones with energy tapping, that something occurred to me:

Erin is a self-improvement junkie. She spends tens of thousands of dollars on books and seminars and courses. And the craziest part of all this is that Erin embodies all the lessons she's learned to a T. She has her dream. She stays persistent with it. She visualizes and takes action and weathers the rejections and failures and gets up and tries again. She's relentlessly positive. She thinks pretty damn highly of herself. I mean, she claims to heal cats the same way Jesus healed Lazarus—come the fuck on.

And yet her values are so fucked that none of this matters. The fact that she does everything "right" doesn't make *her* right.

There is a certainty in her that refuses to relinquish itself. She has even told me this in so many words: that she knows her fixation is completely irrational and unhealthy and is making both her and me unhappy. But for some reason it feels so right to her that she can't ignore it and she can't stop.

In the mid-1990s, psychologist Roy Baumeister began researching the concept of evil. Basically, he looked at people who do bad things and at why they do them.

At the time it was assumed that people did bad things because they felt horrible about themselves—that is, they had low self-esteem. One of Baumeister's first surprising findings was that this was often not true. In fact, it was usually the opposite. Some of the worst criminals felt pretty damn good about themselves. And it was this feeling good about themselves in spite of the reality around them that gave them the sense of justification for hurting and disrespecting others.

For individuals to feel justified in doing horrible things to other people, they must feel an unwavering certainty in their own righteousness, in their own beliefs and deservedness. Racists do racist things because they're certain about their genetic superiority. Religious fanatics blow themselves up and murder dozens of people because they're certain of their place in heaven as martyrs. Men rape and abuse women out of their certainty that they're entitled to women's bodies.

Evil people never believe that *they* are evil; rather, they believe that everyone else is evil.

In controversial experiments, now simply known as the Stanford Prison Experiment, organized by the psychologist Philip Zimbardo, researchers told "normal" people that they were to punish other volunteers for breaking various rules. And punish them they did, sometimes escalating the punishment to the point of physical abuse. Almost none of the punishers objected or asked for explanation. On the contrary, many of them seemed to relish the certainty of the moral righteousness bestowed upon them by the experiments.

The problem here is that not only is certainty unattainable, but the pursuit of certainty often breeds more (and worse) insecurity.

Many people have an unshakable certainty in their ability

at their job or in the amount of salary they *should* be making. But that certainty makes them feel worse, not better. They see others getting promoted over them, and they feel slighted. They feel unappreciated and underacknowledged.

Even a behavior as simple as sneaking a peek at your boyfriend's text messages or asking a friend what people are saying about you is driven by insecurity and that aching desire to be certain.

You can check your boyfriend's text messages and find nothing, but that's rarely the end of it; then you may start wondering if he has a second phone. You can feel slighted and stepped over at work to explain why you missed out on a promotion, but then that causes you to distrust your coworkers and second-guess everything they say to you (and how you think they feel about you), which in turn makes you even less likely to get promoted. You can keep pursuing that special someone you're "supposed" to be with, but with each rebuffed advance and each lonely night, you only begin to question more and more what you're doing wrong.

And it's in these moments of insecurity, of deep despair, that we become susceptible to an insidious entitlement: believing that we *deserve* to cheat a little to get our way, that other people *deserve* to be punished, that we *deserve* to take what we want, and sometimes violently.

It's the backwards law again: the more you try to be certain about something, the more uncertain and insecure you will feel.

But the converse is true as well: the more you embrace

being uncertain and not knowing, the more comfortable you will feel in knowing what you don't know.

Uncertainty removes our judgments of others; it preempts the unnecessary stereotyping and biases that we otherwise feel when we see somebody on TV, in the office, or on the street. Uncertainty also relieves us of our judgment of ourselves. We don't know if we're lovable or not; we don't know how attractive we are; we don't know how successful we could potentially become. The only way to achieve these things is to remain uncertain of them and be open to finding them out through experience.

Uncertainty is the root of all progress and all growth. As the old adage goes, the man who believes he knows everything learns nothing. We cannot learn anything without first not knowing something. The more we admit we do not know, the more opportunities we gain to learn.

Our values are imperfect and incomplete, and to assume that they are perfect and complete is to put us in a dangerously dogmatic mindset that breeds entitlement and avoids responsibility. The only way to solve our problems is to first admit that our actions and beliefs up to this point have been wrong and are not working.

This openness to being wrong *must exist* for any real change or growth to take place.

Before we can look at our values and prioritizations and change them into better, healthier ones, we must first become *uncertain* of our current values. We must intellectually strip them away, see their faults and biases, see how they don't fit in with much of the rest of the world, to stare our own ignorance in the face and concede, because our own ignorance is greater than us all.

Manson's Law of Avoidance

Chances are you've heard some form of Parkinson's law: "Work expands so as to fill up the time available for its completion."

You've also undoubtedly heard of Murphy's law: "Whatever can go wrong will go wrong."

Well, next time you're at a swanky cocktail party and you want to impress somebody, try dropping Manson's law of avoidance on them:

> The more something threatens your identity, the more you will avoid it.

That means the more something threatens to change how you view yourself, how successful/unsuccessful you believe yourself to be, how well you see yourself living up to your values, the more you will avoid ever getting around to doing it.

There's a certain comfort that comes with knowing how you fit in the world. Anything that shakes up that comfort— even if it could potentially make your life better—is inherently scary.

Manson's law applies to both good and bad things in life. Making a million dollars could threaten your identity just as much as losing all your money; becoming a famous rock star could threaten your identity just as much as losing your job. This is why people are often so afraid of success—for the exact same reason they're afraid of failure: it threatens who they believe themselves to be.

You avoid writing that screenplay you've always dreamed of because doing so would call into question your identity as a practical insurance adjuster. You avoid talking to your husband about being more adventurous in the bedroom because that conversation would challenge your identity as a good, moral woman. You avoid telling your friend that you don't want to see him anymore because ending the friendship would conflict with your identity as a nice, forgiving person.

These are good, important opportunities that we consistently pass up because they threaten to change how we view and feel about ourselves. They threaten the values that we've chosen and have learned to live up to.

I had a friend who, for the longest time, talked about putting his artwork online and trying to make a go of it as a professional (or at least semiprofessional) artist. He talked about it for years; he saved up money; he even built a few different websites and uploaded his portfolio.

But he never launched. There was always some reason: the resolution on his work wasn't good enough, or he had just painted something better, or he wasn't in a position to dedicate enough time to it yet.

Years passed and he never did give up his "real job." Why? Because despite dreaming about making a living through his art, the real potential of becoming An Artist Nobody Likes was far, far scarier than remaining An Artist Nobody's

Heard Of. At least he was comfortable with and used to being An Artist Nobody's Heard Of.

I had another friend who was a party guy, always going out drinking and chasing girls. After years of living the "high life," he found himself terribly lonely, depressed, and unhealthy. He wanted to give up his party lifestyle. He spoke with a fierce jealousy of those of us who were in relationships and more "settled down" than he was. Yet he never changed. For years he went on, empty night after empty night, bottle after bottle. Always some excuse. Always some reason he couldn't slow down.

Giving up that lifestyle threatened his identity too much. The Party Guy was all he knew how to be. To give that up would be like committing psychological hara-kiri.

We all have values for ourselves. We protect these values. We try to live up to them and we justify them and maintain them. Even if we don't mean to, that's how our brain is wired. As noted before, we're unfairly biased toward what we already know, what we believe to be certain. If I believe I'm a nice guy, I'll avoid situations that could potentially contradict that belief. If I believe I'm an awesome cook, I'll seek out opportunities to prove that to myself over and over again. The belief always takes precedence. Until we change how we view ourselves, what we believe we are and are not, we cannot overcome our avoidance and anxiety. We cannot change.

In this way, "knowing yourself" or "finding yourself" can be dangerous. It can cement you into a strict role and saddle you with unnecessary expectations. It can close you off to inner potential and outer opportunities.

I say *don't* find yourself. I say *never* know who you are. Because that's what keeps you striving and discovering. And it forces you to remain humble in your judgments and accepting of the differences in others.

Kill Yourself

Buddhism argues that your idea of who "you" are is an arbitrary mental construction and that you should let go of the idea that "you" exist at all; that the arbitrary metrics by which you define yourself actually trap you, and thus you're better off letting go of everything. In a sense, you could say that Buddhism encourages you to not give a fuck.

It sounds wonky, but there are some psychological benefits to this approach to life. When we let go of the stories we tell about ourselves, to ourselves, we free ourselves up to actually act (and fail) and grow.

When someone admits to herself, "You know, maybe I'm not good at relationships," then she is suddenly free to act and end her bad marriage. She has no identity to protect by staying in a miserable, crappy marriage just to prove something to herself.

When the student admits to himself, "You know, maybe I'm not a rebel; maybe I'm just scared," then he's free to be ambitious again. He has no reason to feel threatened by pursuing his academic dreams and maybe failing.

When the insurance adjuster admits to himself, "You

know, maybe there's nothing unique or special about my dreams or my job," then he's free to give that screenplay an honest go and see what happens.

I have both some good news and some bad news for you: *there is little that is unique or special about your problems.* That's why letting go is so liberating.

There's a kind of self-absorption that comes with fear based on an irrational certainty. When you assume that your plane is the one that's going to crash, or that your project idea is the stupid one everyone is going to laugh at, or that you're the one everyone is going to choose to mock or ignore, you're implicitly telling yourself, "I'm the exception; I'm unlike everybody else; I'm different and special."

This is narcissism, pure and simple. You feel as though *your* problems deserve to be treated differently, that *your* problems have some unique math to them that doesn't obey the laws of the physical universe.

My recommendation: *don't* be special; *don't* be unique. Redefine your metrics in mundane and broad ways. Choose to measure yourself not as a rising star or an undiscovered genius. Choose to measure yourself not as some horrible victim or dismal failure. Instead, measure yourself by more mundane identities: a student, a partner, a friend, a creator.

The narrower and rarer the identity you choose for yourself, the more everything will seem to threaten you. For that reason, define yourself in the simplest and most ordinary ways possible.

This often means giving up some grandiose ideas about

yourself: that you're uniquely intelligent, or spectacularly talented, or intimidatingly attractive, or especially victimized in ways other people could never imagine. This means giving up your sense of entitlement and your belief that you're somehow owed something by this world. This means giving up the supply of emotional highs that you've been sustaining yourself on for years. Like a junkie giving up the needle, you're going to go through withdrawal when you start giving these things up. But you'll come out the other side so much better.

How to Be a Little Less Certain of Yourself

Questioning ourselves and doubting our own thoughts and beliefs is one of the hardest skills to develop. But it can be done. Here are some questions that will help you breed a little more uncertainty in your life.

Question #1: What if I'm wrong?

A friend of mine recently got engaged to be married. The guy who proposed to her is pretty solid. He doesn't drink. He doesn't hit her or mistreat her. He's friendly and has a good job.

But since the engagement, my friend's brother has been admonishing her nonstop about her immature life choices, warning her that she's going to hurt herself with this guy, that she's making a mistake, that she's being irresponsible. And whenever my friend asks her brother, "What is your problem? Why does this bother you so much?" he acts as though there *is* no problem, that nothing about the engagement bothers him, that he's just trying to be helpful and look out for his little sister.

But it's clear that something *does* bother him. Perhaps it's his own insecurities about getting married. Perhaps it's a sibling rivalry thing. Perhaps it's jealousy. Perhaps he's just so caught up in his own victimhood that he doesn't know how to show happiness for others without trying to make them feel miserable first.

As a general rule, we're all the world's worst observers of ourselves. When we're angry, or jealous, or upset, we're oftentimes the last ones to figure it out. And the only way to figure it out is to put cracks in our armor of certainty by consistently questioning how wrong we might be about ourselves.

"Am I jealous—and if I am, then why?" "Am I angry?" "Is she right, and I'm just protecting my ego?"

Questions like these need to become a mental habit. In many cases, the simple act of asking ourselves such questions generates the humility and compassion needed to resolve a lot of our issues.

But it's important to note that just because you ask yourself if you have the wrong idea doesn't necessarily mean that you do. If your husband beats the crap out of you for burning the pot roast and you ask yourself if you're wrong to believe he's mistreating you—well, sometimes you're right. The goal is merely to ask the question and entertain the thought at the moment, not to hate yourself.

It's worth remembering that for any change to happen

in your life, *you must be wrong about something.* If you're sitting there, miserable day after day, then that means you're *already wrong* about something major in your life, and until you're able to question yourself to find it, nothing will change.

Question #2: What would it mean if I were wrong?

Many people are able to ask themselves if they're wrong, but few are able to go the extra step and admit what it would *mean* if they were wrong. That's because the potential meaning behind our wrongness is often painful. Not only does it call into question our values, but it forces us to consider what a different, contradictory value could potentially look and feel like.

Aristotle wrote, "It is the mark of an educated mind to be able to entertain a thought without accepting it." Being able to look at and evaluate different values without necessarily adopting them is perhaps *the* central skill required in changing one's own life in a meaningful way.

As for my friend's brother, his question to himself should be, "What would it mean if I were wrong about my sister's wedding?" Often the answer to such a question is pretty straightforward (and some form of "I'm being a selfish/insecure/narcissistic asshole"). If he *is* wrong, and his sister's engagement is fine and healthy and happy, there's really no way to explain his own behavior other than through his own insecurities and fucked-up values. He assumes that he knows what's best for his sister and that she can't make major life decisions for herself; he assumes that he has the right and responsibility to make decisions for her; he is certain that he's right and everyone else must be wrong.

Even once uncovered, whether in my friend's brother or in ourselves, that sort of entitlement is hard to admit. It hurts. That's why few people ask the difficult questions. But probing questions are necessary in order to get at the core problems that are motivating his, and our, dickish behavior.

Question #3: Would being wrong create a better or a worse problem than my current problem, for both myself and others?

This is the litmus test for determining whether we've got some pretty solid values going on, or we're totally neurotic fuckwads taking our fucks out on everyone, including ourselves.

The goal here is to look at which *problem* is better. Because after all, as Disappointment Panda said, life's problems are endless.

My friend's brother, what are his options?

A. Continue causing drama and friction within the family, complicating what should otherwise be a happy moment, and damage the trust and respect he has with his sister, all because he has a hunch (some might call it an intuition) that this guy is bad for her.

B. Mistrust his own ability to determine what's right or wrong for his sister's life and remain humble, trust her ability to make her own decisions, and even if he doesn't, live with the results out of his love and respect for her.

Most people choose option A. That's because option A is the easier path. It requires little thought, no second-guessing, and zero tolerance of decisions other people make that you don't like.

It also creates the most misery for everyone involved.

It's option B that sustains healthy and happy relationships built on trust and respect. It's option B that forces people to remain humble and admit ignorance. It's option B that allows people to grow beyond their insecurities and recognize situations where they're being impulsive or unfair or selfish.

But option B is hard and painful, so most people don't choose it.

My friend's brother, in protesting her engagement, entered into an imaginary battle with himself. Sure, he believed he was trying to protect his sister, but as we've seen, beliefs are arbitrary; worse yet, they're often made up after the fact to justify whatever values and metrics we've chosen for ourselves. The truth is, he would rather fuck up his relationship with his sister than consider that he might be wrong—even though the latter could help him to grow out of the insecurities that made him wrong in the first place.

I try to live with few rules, but one that I've adopted over the years is this: if it's down to me being screwed up, or everybody else being screwed up, it is far, far, far more likely that I'm the one who's screwed up. I have learned this from experience. I have been the asshole acting out based on my own insecurities and flawed certainties more times than I can count. It's not pretty.

That's not to say there aren't certain ways in which most people are screwed up. And that's not to say that there aren't times when you'll be more right than most other people.

That's simply reality: if it feels like it's you versus the world, chances are it's really just you versus yourself.

CHAPTER

7

Failure Is the Way Forward

really mean it when I say it: I was fortunate.

I graduated college in 2007, just in time for the financial collapse and Great Recession, and attempted to enter the worst job market in more than eighty years.

Around the same time, I found out that the person who was subletting one of the rooms in my apartment hadn't paid any rent for three months. When confronted about this, she cried and then disappeared, leaving my other roommate and me to cover everything. Goodbye, savings. I spent the next six months living on a friend's couch, stringing together odd jobs and trying to stay in as little debt as possible while looking for a "real job."

I say I was fortunate because I entered the adult world already a failure. I started out at rock bottom. That's basically everybody's biggest fear later on in life, when confronted with starting a new business or changing careers or quitting an awful job, and I got to experience it right out of the gates. Things could only get better.

So yeah, lucky. When you're sleeping on a smelly futon and have to count coins to figure out whether you can afford McDonald's this week and you've sent out twenty résumés without hearing a single word back, then starting a blog and a stupid Internet business doesn't sound like such a scary idea. If every project I started failed, if every post I wrote went unread, I'd only be back exactly where I started. So why not try?

Failure itself is a relative concept. If my metric had been to become an anarcho-communist revolutionary, then my complete failure to make any money between 2007 and 2008 would have been a raving success. But if, like most people, my metric had been to simply find a first serious job that could pay some bills right out of school, I was a dismal failure.

I grew up in a wealthy family. Money was never a problem. On the contrary, I grew up in a wealthy family where money was more often used to avoid problems than solve them. I was again fortunate, because this taught me at an early age that making money, by itself, was a lousy metric for myself. You could make plenty of money and be miserable, just as you could be broke and be pretty happy. Therefore, why use money as a means to measure my self-worth?

Instead, my value was something else. It was freedom, autonomy. The idea of being an entrepreneur had always appealed to me because I hated being told what to do and preferred to do things my way. The idea of working on the Internet appealed to me because I could do it from anywhere and work whenever I wanted.

I asked myself a simple question: "Would I rather make decent money and work a job I hated, or play at Internet entrepreneur and be broke for a while?" The answer was immediate and clear for me: the latter. I then asked myself, "If I try this thing and fail in a few years and have to go get a job anyway, will I have really lost anything?" The answer was no. Instead of a broke and unemployed twenty-two-year-old with no experience, I'd be a broke and unemployed twenty-five-year-old with no experience. Who cares?

With this value, to *not* pursue my own projects became the failure—not a lack of money, not sleeping on friends' and family's couches (which I continued to do for most of the next two years), and not an empty résumé.

The Failure/Success Paradox

When Pablo Picasso was an old man, he was sitting in a café in Spain, doodling on a used napkin. He was nonchalant about the whole thing, drawing whatever amused him in that moment—kind of the same way teenage boys draw penises on bathroom stalls—except this was Picasso, so his bathroom-stall penises were more like cubist/impressionist awesomeness laced on top of faint coffee stains.

Anyway, some woman sitting near him was looking on in awe. After a few moments, Picasso finished his coffee and crumpled up the napkin to throw away as he left.

The woman stopped him. "Wait," she said. "Can I have that napkin you were just drawing on? I'll pay you for it."

"Sure," Picasso replied. "Twenty thousand dollars."

The woman's head jolted back as if he had just flung a brick at her. "What? It took you like two minutes to draw that."

"No, ma'am," Picasso said. "It took me over sixty years to draw this." He stuffed the napkin in his pocket and walked out of the café.

Improvement at anything is based on thousands of tiny failures, and the magnitude of your success is based on how many times you've failed at something. If someone is better than you at something, then it's likely because she has failed at it more than you have. If someone is worse than you, it's likely because he hasn't been through all of the painful learning experiences you have.

If you think about a young child trying to learn to walk, that child will fall down and hurt itself hundreds of times. But at no point does that child ever stop and think, "Oh, I guess walking just isn't for me. I'm not good at it."

Avoiding failure is something we learn at some later point in life. I'm sure a lot of it comes from our education system, which judges rigorously based on performance and punishes those who don't do well. Another large share of it comes from overbearing or critical parents who don't let their kids screw up on their own often enough, and instead punish them for trying anything new or not preordained. And then we have all the mass media that constantly expose us to stellar success after success, while not showing us the thousands of hours of dull practice and tedium that were required to achieve that success.

At some point, most of us reach a place where we're afraid to fail, where we instinctively avoid failure and stick only to what is placed in front of us or only what we're already good at.

This confines us and stifles us. We can be truly successful only at something we're willing to fail at. If we're unwilling to fail, then we're unwilling to succeed.

A lot of this fear of failure comes from having chosen shitty values. For instance, if I measure myself by the standard "Make everyone I meet like me," I will be anxious, because failure is 100 percent defined by the actions of others, not by my own actions. I am not in control; thus my self-worth is at the mercy of judgments by others.

Whereas if I instead adopt the metric "Improve my social life," I can live up to my value of "good relations with others" regardless of how other people respond to me. My self-worth is based on my own behaviors and happiness.

Shitty values, as we saw in chapter 4, involve tangible external goals outside of our control. The pursuit of these goals causes great anxiety. And even if we manage to achieve them, they leave us feeling empty and lifeless, because once they're achieved there are no more problems to solve.

Better values, as we saw, are process-oriented. Something like "Express myself honestly to others," a metric for the value "honesty," is never completely finished; it's a problem that must continuously be reengaged. Every new conversation, every new relationship, brings new challenges and opportunities for honest expression. The value is an ongoing, lifelong process that defies completion.

If your metric for the value "success by worldly standards" is "Buy a house and a nice car," and you spend twenty years working your ass off to achieve it, once it's achieved the metric has nothing left to give you. Then say hello to your midlife crisis, because the problem that drove you your entire adult life was just taken away from you. There are no other opportunities to keep growing and improving, and yet it's growth that generates happiness, not a long list of arbitrary achievements.

In this sense, goals, as they are conventionally defined— graduate from college, buy a lake house, lose fifteen pounds—are limited in the amount of happiness they can produce in our lives. They may be helpful when pursuing quick, short-term benefits, but as guides for the overall trajectory of our life, they suck.

Picasso remained prolific his entire life. He lived into his nineties and continued to produce art up until his final years. Had his metric been "Become famous" or "Make a buttload of money in the art world" or "Paint one thousand pictures," he would have stagnated at some point along the way. He would have been overcome by anxiety or self-doubt. He likely wouldn't have improved and innovated his craft in the ways he did decade after decade.

The reason for Picasso's success is exactly the same reason why, as an old man, he was happy to scribble drawings on a napkin alone in a café. His underlying value was simple and humble. And it was endless. It was the value "honest ex-pression." And this is what made that napkin so valuable.

Pain Is Part of the Process

In the 1950s, a Polish psychologist named Kazimierz Dabrowski studied World War II survivors and how they'd coped with traumatic experiences in the war. This was Poland, so things had been pretty gruesome. These people had experienced or witnessed mass starvation, bombings that turned cities to rubble, the Holocaust, the torture of prisoners of war, and the rape and/or murder of family members, if not by the Nazis, then a few years later by the Soviets.

As Dabrowski studied the survivors, he noticed some-thing both surprising and amazing. A sizable percentage of them believed that the wartime experiences they'd suf-fered, although painful and indeed traumatic, had actually caused them to become better, more responsible, and yes, even happier people. Many described their lives before the war as if they'd been different people then: ungrateful for and unappreciative of their loved ones, lazy and consumed by petty problems, entitled to all they'd been given. After the war they felt more confident, more sure of themselves, more grateful, and unfazed by life's trivialities and petty annoyances.

Obviously, their experiences had been horrific, and these survivors weren't happy about having had to experience them. Many of them still suffered from the emotional scars the lashings of war had left on them. But some of them had managed to leverage those scars to transform themselves in positive and powerful ways.

And they aren't alone in that reversal. For many of us, our proudest achievements come in the face of the greatest adversity. Our pain often makes us stronger, more resilient, more grounded. Many cancer survivors, for example, report feeling stronger and more grateful after winning their battle to survive. Many military personnel report a mental resilience gained from withstanding the dangerous environments of being in a war zone.

Dabrowski argued that fear and anxiety and sadness are not necessarily always undesirable or unhelpful states of mind; rather, they are often representative of the necessary pain of psychological growth. And to deny that pain is to deny our own potential. Just as one must suffer physical pain to build stronger bone and muscle, one must suffer emotional pain to develop greater emotional resilience, a stronger sense of self, increased compassion, and a generally happier life.

Our most radical changes in perspective often happen at the tail end of our worst moments. It's only when we feel intense pain that we're willing to look at our values and question why they seem to be failing us. We *need* some sort of existential crisis to take an objective look at how we've been deriving meaning in our life, and then consider changing course.

You could call it "hitting bottom" or "having an existential crisis." I prefer to call it "weathering the shitstorm." Choose what suits you.

And perhaps you're in that kind of place right now. Perhaps you're coming out of the most significant challenge of your life and are bewildered because everything you previously thought to be true and normal and good has turned out to be the opposite.

That's good—that's the beginning. I can't stress this enough, but *pain is part of the process*. It's important to *feel* it. Because if you just chase after highs to cover up the pain, if you continue to indulge in entitlement and delusional positive thinking, if you continue to overindulge in various substances or activities, then you'll never generate the requisite motivation to actually change.

When I was young, any time my family got a new VCR or stereo, I would press every button, plug and unplug every cord and cable, just to see what everything did. With time, I learned how the whole system worked. And because I knew how it all worked, I was often the only person in the house who used the stuff.

As is the case for many millennial children, my parents looked on as if I were some sort of prodigy. To them, the fact that I could program the VCR without looking at the instruction manual made me the Second Coming of Tesla.

It's easy to look back at my parents' generation and chuckle at their technophobia. But the further I get into adulthood, the more I realize that we all have areas of our lives where we're like my parents with the new VCR: we sit and stare and shake our heads and say, "But *how*?" When really, it's as simple as just doing it.

I get emails from people asking questions like this all the

time. And for many years, I never knew what to say to them.

There's the girl whose parents are immigrants and saved for their whole lives to put her through med school. But now she's in med school and she hates it; she doesn't want to spend her life as a doctor, so she wants to drop out more than anything. Yet she feels stuck. So stuck, in fact, that she ends up emailing a stranger on the Internet (me) and asking him a silly and obvious question like, "How do I drop out of med school?"

Or the college guy who has a crush on his tutor. So he agonizes over every sign, every laugh, every smile, every diversion into small talk, and emails me a twenty-eight-page novella that concludes with the question, "How do I ask her out?" Or the single mother whose now-adult kids have finished school and are loafing around on her couch, eating her food, spending her money, not respecting her space or her desire for privacy. She wants them to move on with their lives. She wants to move on with *her* life. Yet she's scared to death of pushing her children away, scared to the point of asking, "How do I ask them to move out?"

These are VCR questions. From the outside, the answer is simple: just shut up and do it.

But from the inside, from the perspective of each of these people, these questions feel impossibly complex and opaque—existential riddles wrapped in enigmas packed in a KFC bucket full of Rubik's Cubes.

VCR questions are funny because the answer appears difficult to anyone who has them and appears easy to anyone who does not.

The problem here is pain. Filling out the appropriate paperwork to drop out of med school is a straightforward and obvious action; breaking your parents' hearts is not. Asking a tutor out on a date is as simple as saying the words; risking intense embarrassment and rejection feels far more complicated. Asking someone to move out of your house is a clear decision; feeling as if you're abandoning your own children is not.

I struggled with social anxiety throughout much of my adolescence and young adult life. I spent most of my days distracting myself with video games and most of my nights either drinking or smoking away my uneasiness. For many years, the thought of speaking to a stranger—especially if that stranger happened to be particularly attractive/interesting/popular/smart—felt impossible to me. I walked around in a daze for years, asking myself dumb VCR questions:

"How? How do you just walk up and talk to a person? How can somebody *do* that?"

I had all sorts of screwed-up beliefs about this, like that you weren't allowed to speak to someone unless you had some practical reason to, or that women would think I was a creepy rapist if I so much as said, "Hello."

The problem was that my emotions defined my reality. Because it *felt* like people didn't want to talk to me, I came to *believe* that people didn't want to talk to me. And thus, my VCR question: "How do you just walk up and talk to a person?"

Because I failed to separate what I *felt* from what *was*, I was incapable of stepping outside myself and seeing the world for what it was: a simple place where two people can walk up to each other at any time and speak.

Many people, when they feel some form of pain or anger or sadness, drop everything and attend to numbing out whatever they're feeling. Their goal is to get back to "feeling good" again as quickly as possible, even if that means substances or deluding themselves or returning to their shitty values.

Learn to sustain the pain you've chosen. When you choose a new value, you are choosing to introduce a new form of pain into your life. Relish it. Savor it. Welcome it with open arms. Then act *despite* it.

I won't lie: this is going to feel impossibly hard at first. But you can start simple. You're going to feel as though you don't know what to do. But we've discussed this: you don't know *anything*. Even when you think you do, you really don't know what the fuck you're doing. So really, what is there to lose?

Life is about not knowing and then doing something anyway. *All* of life is like this. It never changes. Even when you're happy. Even when you're farting fairy dust. Even when you win the lottery and buy a small fleet of Jet Skis, you still won't know what the hell you're doing. Don't ever forget that. And don't ever be afraid of that.

The "Do Something" Principle

In 2008, after holding down a day job for all of six weeks, I gave up on the whole job thing to pursue an online business.

At the time, I had absolutely no clue what I was doing, but I figured if I was going to be broke and miserable, I might as well be while working on my own terms. And at that time, all I seemed to really care about was chasing girls. So fuck it, I decided to start a blog about my crazy dating life.

That first morning that I woke up self-employed, terror quickly consumed me. I found myself sitting with my laptop and realized, for the first time, that I was entirely responsible for *all* of my own decisions, as well as the consequences of those decisions. I was responsible for teaching myself web design, Internet marketing, search engine optimization, and other esoteric topics. It was all on my shoulders now. And so I did what any twenty-four-year-old who'd just quit his job and had no idea what he was doing would do: I downloaded some computer games and avoided work like it was the Ebola virus.

As the weeks went on and my bank account turned from black to red, it was clear that I needed to come up with some sort of strategy to get myself to put in the twelve- or fourteen-hour days that were necessary to get a new business off the ground. And that plan came from an unexpected place.

When I was in high school, my math teacher Mr. Packwood used to say, "If you're stuck on a problem, don't sit there and think about it; just start working on it. Even if you don't know what you're doing, the simple act of working on it will eventually cause the right ideas to show up in your head."

During that early self-employment period, when I struggled every day, completely clueless about what to do and terrified of the results (or lack thereof), Mr. Packwood's advice started beckoning me from the recesses of my mind. I heard it like a mantra:

> Don't just sit there. *Do* something. The answers will follow.

In the course of applying Mr. Packwood's advice, I learned a powerful lesson about motivation. It took about eight years for this lesson to sink in, but what I discovered, over those long, grueling months of bombed product launches, laughable advice columns, uncomfortable nights on friends' couches, overdrawn bank accounts, and hundreds of thousands of words written (most of them unread), was perhaps the most important thing I've ever learned in my life:

> Action isn't just the effect of motivation; it's also the cause of it.

Most of us commit to action only if we feel a certain level of motivation. And we feel motivation only when we feel enough emotional inspiration. We assume that these steps occur in a sort of chain reaction, like this:

> Emotional inspiration → Motivation → Desirable action

If you want to accomplish something but don't feel motivated or inspired, then you assume you're just screwed. There's nothing you can do about it. It's not until a major emotional life event occurs that you can generate enough motivation to actually get off the couch and do something.

The thing about motivation is that it's not only a three-part chain, but an endless loop:

Inspiration → Motivation → Action → Inspiration
→ Motivation → Action → Etc.

Your actions create further emotional reactions and inspirations and move on to motivate your future actions. Taking advantage of this knowledge, we can actually reorient our mindset in the following way: \

Action → Inspiration → Motivation

If you lack the motivation to make an important change in your life, *do something*—anything, really—and then harness the reaction to that action as a way to begin motivating yourself.

I call this the "do something" principle. After using it myself to build my business, I began teaching it to readers who came to me perplexed by their own VCR questions: "How do I apply for a job?" or "How do I tell this guy I want to be his girlfriend?" and the like.

During the first couple years I worked for myself, entire weeks would go by without my accomplishing much, for no other reason than that I was anxious and stressed about what I had to do, and it was too easy to put everything off. I quickly learned, though, that forcing myself to do *something*, even the most menial of tasks, quickly made the larger tasks seem much easier. If I had to redesign an entire website, I'd force myself to sit down and would say, "Okay, I'll just design the header right now." But after the header was done, I'd find myself moving on to other parts of the site. And before I knew it, I'd be energized and engaged in the project.

The author Tim Ferriss relates a story he once heard about a novelist who had written over seventy novels. Someone asked the novelist how he was able to write so consistently and remain inspired and motivated. He replied, "Two hundred crappy words per day, that's it." The idea was that if he forced himself to write two hundred crappy words, more often than not the act of writing would inspire him; and before he knew it, he'd have thousands of words down on the page.

If we follow the "do something" principle, failure *feels* unimportant. When the standard of success becomes merely acting—when *any* result is regarded as progress and important, when inspiration is seen as a reward rather than a prerequisite—we propel ourselves ahead. We feel free to fail, and that failure moves us forward.

The "do something" principle not only helps us overcome procrastination, but it's also the process by which we adopt new values. If you're in the midst of an existential shitstorm and everything feels meaningless—if all the ways you used to measure yourself have come up short and you have no idea what's next, if you know that you've been hurting yourself chasing false dreams, or if you know that there's some better metric you should be measuring yourself with but you don't know how—the answer is the same:

Do something.

That "something" can be the smallest viable action toward something else. It can be *anything*.

Recognize that you've been an entitled prick in all of your relationships and want to start developing more compassion for others? Do something. Start simple. Make it a goal to listen to someone's problem and give some of your time to helping that person. Just do it once. Or promise yourself that you will assume that *you* are the root of your problems next time you get upset. Just try on the idea and see how it feels.

That's often all that's necessary to get the snowball rolling, the action needed to inspire the motivation to keep going. You can become your own source of inspiration. You can become your own source of motivation. Action is always within reach. And with simply *doing something* as your only metric for success—well, then even failure pushes you forward.

The Importance of Saying No

I n 2009, I gathered up all my possessions, sold them or put them into storage, left my apartment, and set off for Latin America. By this time my little dating advice blog was getting some traffic and I was actually making a modest amount of money selling PDFs and courses online. I planned on spending much of the next few years living abroad, experiencing new cultures, and taking advantage of the lower cost of living in a number of developing countries in Asia and Latin America to build my business further. It was the digital nomad dream and as a twenty-five-year-old adventure-seeker, it was exactly what I wanted out of life.

But as sexy and heroic as my plan sounded, not all of the values driving me to this nomadic lifestyle were healthy ones. Sure, I had some admirable values going on—a thirst to see the world, a curiosity for people and culture, some old-fashioned adventure-seeking. But there also existed a faint outline of shame underlying everything else. At the time I was hardly aware of it, but if I was completely honest with myself, I knew there was a screwed-up value lurking there, somewhere beneath the surface. I couldn't see it, but in quiet moments when I was completely honest with myself, I could feel it.

Along with the entitlement of my early twenties, the "real traumatic shit" of my teenage years had left me with a nice bundle of commitment issues. I had spent the past few years overcompensating for the inadequacy and social anxiety of my teenager years, and as a result I felt like I could meet anybody I wanted, be friends with anybody I wanted, love anybody I wanted, have sex with anybody I wanted— so why would I ever commit to a single person, or even a single social group, a single city or country or culture? If I *could* experience everything equally, then I *should* experience them all equally, right?

Armed with this grandiose sense of connectivity to the world, I bounced back and forth across countries and oceans in a game of global hopscotch that lasted over five years. I visited fifty-five countries, made dozens of friends, and found myself in the arms of a number of lovers—all of whom were quickly replaced and some of whom were already forgotten by the next flight to the next country.

It was a strange life, replete with fantastic, horizon-breaching experiences as well as superficial highs designed to numb my underlying pain. It seemed both so profound yet so meaningless at the same time, and still does. Some of my greatest life lessons and character-defining moments came on the road during this period. But some of the biggest wastes of my time and energy came during this period as well.

Now I live in New York. I have a house and furniture and an electric bill and a wife. None of it is particularly glamorous or exciting. And I like it that way. Because after all the years of excitement, the biggest lesson I took from my adventuring was this: absolute freedom, by itself, means nothing.

Freedom grants the opportunity for greater meaning, but by itself there is nothing necessarily meaningful about it. Ultimately, the only way to achieve meaning and a sense of importance in one's life is through a rejection of alternatives, a *narrowing* of freedom, a choice of commitment to one place, one belief, or (gulp) one person.

This realization came to me slowly over the course of my years traveling. As with most excesses in life, you have to drown yourself in them to realize that they don't make you happy. Such was traveling with me. As I drowned in my fifty-third, fifty-fourth, fifty-fifth country, I began to understand that while all of my experiences were exciting and great, few of them would have any lasting significance. Whereas my friends back home were settling down into marriages, buying houses, and giving their time to interesting companies or political causes, I was floundering from one high to the next.

In 2011, I traveled to Saint Petersburg, Russia. The food sucked. The weather sucked. (Snow in May? Are you fucking kidding me?) My apartment sucked. Nothing worked. Everything was overpriced. The people were rude and smelled funny. Nobody smiled and everyone drank too much. Yet, I loved it. It was one of my favorite trips.

There's a bluntness to Russian culture that generally rubs Westerners the wrong way. Gone are the fake niceties and verbal webs of politeness. You don't smile at strangers or pretend to like anything you don't. In Russia, if something is stupid, you say it's stupid. If someone is being an asshole, you tell him he's being an asshole. If you really like someone and are having a great time, you tell her that you like her and are having a great time. It doesn't matter if this person is your friend, a stranger, or someone you met five minutes ago on the street.

The first week I found all of this really uncomfortable. I went on a coffee date with a Russian girl, and within three minutes of sitting down she looked at me funny and told me that what I'd just said was stupid. I nearly choked on my drink. There was nothing combative about the way she said it; it was spoken as if it were some mundane fact—like the quality of the weather that day, or her shoe size—but I was still shocked. After all, in the West such outspokenness is seen as highly offensive, especially from someone you just met. But it went on like this with everyone. Everyone came across as rude all the time, and as a result, my Western-coddled mind felt attacked on all sides. Nagging insecurities began to surface in situations where they hadn't existed in years.

But as the weeks wore on, I got used to the Russian

frankness, much as I did the midnight sunsets and the vodka that went down like ice water. And then I started appreciating it for what it really was: unadulterated expression. Honesty in the truest sense of the word. Communication with no conditions, no strings attached, no ulterior motive, no sales job, no desperate attempt to be liked.

Somehow, after years of travel, it was in perhaps the most un-American of places where I first experienced a particular flavor of freedom: the ability to say whatever I thought or felt, without fear of repercussion. It was a strange form of liberation *through* accepting rejection. And as someone who had been starved of this kind of blunt expression most of his life—first by an emotionally repressed family life, then later by a meticulously constructed false display of confidence—I got drunk on it like, well, like it was the finest damn vodka I'd ever had. The month I spent in Saint Petersburg went by in a blur, and by the end I didn't want to leave.

Travel is a fantastic self-development tool, because it extricates you from the values of your culture and shows you that another society can live with entirely different values and still function and not hate themselves. This exposure to different cultural values and metrics then forces you to reexamine what seems obvious in your own life and to consider that perhaps it's not necessarily the best way to live. In this case, Russia had me reexamining the bullshitty, fake-nice communication that is so common in Anglo culture, and asking myself if this wasn't somehow making us more insecure around each other and worse at intimacy.

I remember discussing this dynamic with my Russian teacher one day, and he had an interesting theory. Having lived under communism for so many generations, with little to no economic opportunity and caged by a culture of fear, Russian society found the most valuable currency to be trust. And to build trust you have to be honest. That means when things suck, you say so openly and without apology. People's displays of unpleasant honesty were rewarded for the simple fact that they were necessary for survival—you had to know whom you could rely on and whom you couldn't, and you needed to know quickly.

But, in the "free" West, my Russian teacher continued, there existed an abundance of economic opportunity—so much economic opportunity that it became far more valuable to present yourself in a certain way, even if it was false, than to actually *be* that way. Trust lost its value. Appearances and salesmanship became more advantageous forms of expression. Knowing a lot of people superficially was more beneficial than knowing a few people closely.

This is why it became the norm in Western cultures to smile and say polite things even when you don't feel like it, to tell little white lies and agree with someone whom you don't actually agree with. This is why people learn to pretend to be friends with people they don't actually like, to buy things they don't actually want. The economic system promotes such deception.

The downside of this is that you never know, in the West, if you can completely trust the person you're talking to. Sometimes this is the case even among good friends or family members. There is such pressure in the West to be likable that people often reconfigure their entire personality depending on the person they're dealing with.

Rejection Makes Your Life Better

As an extension of our positivity/consumer culture, many of us have been "indoctrinated" with the belief that we should try to be as inherently accepting and affirmative as possible. This is a cornerstone of many of the so-called positive thinking books: open yourself up to opportunities, be accepting, say yes to everything and everyone, and so on.

But we *need* to reject something. Otherwise, we stand for nothing. If nothing is better or more desirable than anything else, then we are empty and our life is meaningless. We are without values and therefore live our life without any purpose.

The avoidance of rejection (both giving and receiving it) is often sold to us as a way to make ourselves feel better. But avoiding rejection gives us short-term pleasure by making us rudderless and directionless in the long term.

To truly appreciate something, you must confine yourself to it. There's a certain level of joy and meaning that you reach in life only when you've spent decades investing in a single relationship, a single craft, a single career. And you cannot achieve those decades of investment without rejecting the alternatives.

The act of choosing a value for yourself requires rejecting alternative values. If I choose to make my marriage the most important part of my life, that means I'm (probably) choosing *not* to make cocaine-fueled hooker orgies an important part of my life. If I'm choosing to judge myself based on my ability to have open and accepting friendships, that means I'm rejecting trashing my friends behind their backs. These are all healthy decisions, yet they require rejection at every turn.

The point is this: we all must give a fuck about *something,* in order to *value* something. And to value something, we must reject what is *not* that something. To value X, we must reject non-X.

That rejection is an inherent and necessary part of maintaining our values, and therefore our identity. We are defined by what we choose to reject. And if we reject nothing (perhaps in fear of being rejected by something ourselves), we essentially have no identity at all.

The desire to avoid rejection at all costs, to avoid confrontation and conflict, the desire to attempt to accept everything equally and to make everything cohere and harmonize, is a deep and subtle form of entitlement. Entitled people, because they feel as though they *deserve* to feel great all the time, avoid rejecting anything because doing so might make them or someone else feel bad. And because they refuse to reject anything, they live a valueless, pleasure-driven, and self-absorbed life. All they give a fuck about is sustaining the high a little bit longer, to avoid the inevitable failures of their life, to pretend the suffering away.

Rejection is an important and crucial life skill. Nobody wants to be stuck in a relationship that isn't making them happy. Nobody wants to be stuck in a business doing work they hate and don't believe in. Nobody wants to feel that they can't say what they really mean.

Yet people choose these things. All the time.

Honesty is a natural human craving. But part of having honesty in our lives is becoming comfortable with saying and hearing the word "no." In this way, rejection actually makes our relationships better and our emotional lives healthier.

Boundaries

Once upon a time, there were two youngsters, a boy and a girl. Their families hated each other. But the boy snuck into a party hosted by the girl's family because he was kind of a dick. The girl sees the boy, and angels sing so sweetly to her lady-parts that she instantly falls in love with him. Just like that. And so he sneaks into her garden and they decide to get married *the next freaking day,* because, you know, that's totally practical, especially when your parents want to murder each other. Jump ahead a few days. Their families find out about the marriage and throw a shit-fit. Mercutio dies. The girl is so upset that she drinks a potion that will put her to sleep for two days. But, unfortunately, the young couple hasn't learned the ins and outs of good marital communication yet, and the young girl totally forgets to mention something about it to her new husband. The young man therefore mistakes his new wife's self-induced coma for suicide. He then totally loses his marbles and *he* commits suicide, thinking he's going to be with her in the afterlife or some shit. But then she wakes up from her two-day coma, only to learn that her new husband has committed suicide, so *she* has the exact same idea and kills herself too. The end.

Romeo and Juliet is synonymous with "romance" in our culture today. It is seen as *the* love story in English-speaking culture, an emotional ideal to live up to. Yet when you really get down to what happens in the story, these kids are absolutely out of their fucking minds. And they just killed themselves to prove it!

It's suspected by many scholars that Shakespeare wrote *Romeo and Juliet* not to celebrate romance, but rather to satirize it, to show how absolutely nutty it was. He didn't mean for the play to be a glorification of love. In fact, he meant it to be the opposite: a big flashing neon sign blinking KEEP OUT, with police tape around it saying DO NOT CROSS.

For most of human history, romantic love was not celebrated as it is now. In fact, up until the mid-nineteenth century or so, love was seen as an unnecessary and potentially dangerous psychological impediment to the more important things in life—you know, like farming well and/or marrying a guy with a lot of sheep. Young people were often forcibly steered clear of their romantic passions in favor of practical economic marriages that would yield stability for both them and their families.

But today, we all get brain boners for this kind of batshit crazy love. It dominates our culture. And the more dramatic, the better. Whether it's Ben Affleck working to destroy an asteroid to save the earth for the girl he loves, or Mel Gibson murdering hundreds of Englishmen and fantasizing about his raped and murdered wife while being tortured to death, or that Elven chick giving up her immortality to be with Aragorn in *Lord of the Rings,* or stupid romantic comedies where Jimmy Fallon forgoes his Red Sox playoff tickets because Drew Barrymore has, like, *needs* or something.

If this sort of romantic love were cocaine, then as a culture we'd all be like Tony Montana in *Scarface:* burying our faces in a fucking mountain of it, screaming, "Say hello to my lee-tle friend!"

The problem is that we're finding out that romantic love *is* kind of like cocaine. Like, frighteningly similar to cocaine. Like, stimulates the exact same parts of your brain as cocaine. Like, gets you high and makes you feel good for a while but also creates as many problems as it solves, as does cocaine.

Most elements of romantic love that we pursue—the dramatic and dizzyingly emotional displays of affection, the topsy-turvy ups and downs—aren't healthy, genuine displays of love. In fact, they're often just another form of entitlement playing out through people's relationships.

I know: that makes me sound like such a downer. Seriously, what kind of guy shits on romantic love? But hear me out.

The truth is, there are healthy forms of love and unhealthy forms of love. Unhealthy love is based on two people trying to escape their problems through their emotions for each other—in other words, they're using each other as an escape. Healthy love is based on two people acknowledging and addressing their own problems with each other's support.

The difference between a healthy and an unhealthy relationship comes down to two things: 1) how well each person in the relationship accepts responsibility, and 2) the willingness of each person to both reject and be rejected by their partner.

Anywhere there is an unhealthy or toxic relationship, there will be a poor and porous sense of responsibility on both sides, and there will be an inability to give and/or receive rejection. Wherever there is a healthy and loving relationship, there will be clear boundaries between the two people and their values, and there will be an open avenue of giving and receiving rejection when necessary.

By "boundaries" I mean the delineation between two people's responsibilities for their own problems. People in a healthy relationship with strong boundaries will take responsibility for their own values and problems and not take responsibility for their partner's values and problems. People in a toxic relationship with poor or no boundaries will regularly avoid responsibility for their own problems and/or take responsibility for their partner's problems.

What do poor boundaries look like? Here are some examples:

> *"You can't go out with your friends without me. You*
> *know how jealous I get. You have to stay home*
> *with me."*
> *"My coworkers are idiots; they always make me late to*

*meetings because I have to tell them how to do their
jobs."*

*"I can't believe you made me feel so stupid in front of
my own sister. Never disagree with me in front of her
again!"*

*"I'd love to take that job in Milwaukee, but my mother
would never forgive me for moving so far away."*

*"I can date you, but can you not tell my friend Cindy?
She gets really insecure when I have a boyfriend and
she doesn't."*

In each scenario, the person is either taking responsibility for problems/emotions that are not theirs, or demanding that someone else take responsibility for their problems/emotions.

In general, entitled people fall into one of two traps in their relationships. Either they expect other people to take responsibility for *their* problems: *"I wanted a nice relaxing weekend at home. You should have known that and canceled your plans."* Or they take on too much responsibility for other people's problems: *"She just lost her job again, but it's probably my fault because I wasn't as supportive of her as I could have been. I'm going to help her rewrite her résumé tomorrow."*

Entitled people adopt these strategies in their relationships, as with everything, to help avoid accepting responsibility for their own problems. As a result, their relationships are fragile and fake, products of avoiding inner pain rather than embracing a genuine appreciation and adoration of their partner.

This goes not just for romantic relationships, by the way, but also for family relationships and friendships. An overbearing mother may take responsibility for every problem in her children's lives. Her own entitlement then encourages an entitlement in her children, as they grow up to believe other people should always be responsible for their problems.

(This is why the problems in your romantic relationships always eerily resemble the problems in your parents' relationship.)

When you have murky areas of responsibility for your emotions and actions—areas where it's unclear who is responsible for what, whose fault is what, why you're doing what you're doing—you never develop strong values for yourself. Your only value *becomes* making your partner happy. Or your only value *becomes* your partner making you happy.

This is self-defeating, of course. And relationships characterized by such murkiness usually go down like the *Hindenburg*, with all the drama and fireworks.

People can't solve your problems for you. And they shouldn't try, because that won't make you happy. You can't solve other people's problems for them either, because that likewise won't make them happy. The mark of an unhealthy relationship is two people who try to solve each other's problems in order to feel good about themselves. Rather, a healthy relationship is when two people solve their own problems in order to feel good about each other.

The setting of proper boundaries doesn't mean you can't help or support your partner or be helped and supported yourself. You both should support each other. But only because you *choose* to support and be supported. Not because you feel obligated or entitled.

Entitled people who blame others for their own emotions and actions do so because they believe that if they constantly paint themselves as victims, eventually someone will come along and save them, and they will receive the love they've always wanted.

Entitled people who take the blame for other people's emotions and actions do so because they believe that if they "fix" their partner and save him or her, they will receive the love and appreciation they've always wanted.

These are the yin and yang of any toxic relationship: the victim and the saver, the person who starts fires because it makes her feel important and the person who puts out fires because it makes him feel important.

These two types of people are drawn strongly to one another, and they usually end up together. Their pathologies match one another perfectly. Often they've grown up with parents who each exhibit one of these traits as well. So their model for a "happy" relationship is one based on entitlement and poor boundaries.

Sadly, they both fail in meeting the other's actual needs. In fact, their pattern of overblaming and overaccepting blame perpetuates the entitlement and shitty self-worth that have been keeping them from getting their emotional needs met in the first place. The victim creates more and more problems to solve—not because additional real problems exist, but because it gets her the attention and affection she craves. The saver solves and solves—not because she actually cares about the problems, but because she believes she must fix others' problems in order to deserve attention and affection for herself. In both cases, the intentions are selfish and conditional and therefore self-sabotaging, and genuine love is rarely experienced.

The victim, if he really loved the saver, would say, "Look, this is my problem; you don't have to fix it for me. Just support me while I fix it myself." That would *actually* be a demonstration of love: taking responsibility for your own problems and not holding your partner responsible for them.

If the saver really wanted to save the victim, the saver would say, "Look, you're blaming others for your own problems; deal with this yourself." And in a sick way, that would *actually* be a demonstration of love: helping someone solve their own problems.

Instead, victims and savers both use each other to achieve emotional highs. It's like an addiction they fulfill in one another. Ironically, when presented with emotionally healthy people to date, they usually feel bored or lack "chemistry" with them. They pass on emotionally healthy, secure individuals because the secure partner's solid boundaries don't feel "exciting" enough to stimulate the constant highs necessary in the entitled person.

For victims, the hardest thing to do in the world is to hold themselves accountable for their problems. They've spent their whole life believing that others are responsible for their fate. That first step of taking responsibility for themselves is often terrifying.

For savers, the hardest thing to do in the world is to stop taking responsibility for other people's problems. They've spent their whole life feeling valued and loved only when they're saving somebody else—so letting go of this need is terrifying to them as well.

If you make a sacrifice for someone you care about, it needs to be because you want to, not because you feel obligated or because you fear the consequences of not doing so. If your partner is going to make a sacrifice for you, it needs to be because he or she genuinely wants to, not because you've manipulated the sacrifice through anger or guilt. Acts of love are valid only if they're performed without conditions or expectations.

It can be difficult for people to recognize the difference between doing something out of obligation and doing it voluntarily. So here's a litmus test: ask yourself, "If I refused, how would the relationship change?" Similarly, ask, "If my partner refused something I wanted, how would the relationship change?"

If the answer is that a refusal would cause a blowout of drama and broken china plates, then that's a bad sign for your relationship. It suggests that your relationship is conditional—based on superficial benefits received from one another, rather than on unconditional acceptance of each other (along with each other's problems).

People with strong boundaries are not afraid of a temper tantrum, an argument, or getting hurt. People with weak boundaries are terrified of those things and will constantly mold their own behavior to fit the highs and lows of their relational emotional roller coaster.

People with strong boundaries understand that it's unreasonable to expect two people to accommodate each other 100 percent and fulfill every need the other has. People with strong boundaries understand that they may hurt someone's feelings sometimes, but ultimately they can't determine how other people feel. People with strong boundaries understand that a healthy relationship is not about controlling one another's emotions, but rather about each partner supporting the other in their individual growth and in solving their own problems.

It's not about giving a fuck about everything your partner gives a fuck about; it's about giving a fuck about your partner regardless of the fucks he or she gives. That's unconditional love, baby.

How to Build Trust

My wife is one of those women who spend a lot of time in front of the mirror. She loves to look amazing, and I love for her to look amazing too (obviously).

Nights before we go out, she comes out of the bathroom after an hour-long makeup/hair/clothes/whatever-women-do-in-there session and asks me how she looks. She's usually gorgeous. Every once in a while, though, she looks bad. Maybe she tried to do something new with her hair, or decided to wear a pair of boots that some flamboyant fashion designer from Milan thought were avant-garde. Whatever the reason—it just doesn't work.

When I tell her this, she usually gets pissed off. As she marches back into the closet or the bathroom to redo everything and make us thirty minutes late, she spouts a bunch of four-letter words and sometimes even slings a few of them in my direction.

Men stereotypically lie in this situation to make their girlfriends/wives happy. But I don't. Why? Because honesty in my relationship is more important to me than feeling good all the time. The last person I should ever have to censor myself with is the woman I love.

Fortunately, I'm married to a woman who agrees and is willing to hear my uncensored thoughts. She calls me out on my bullshit too, of course, which is one of the most important traits she offers me as a partner. Sure, my ego gets bruised sometimes, and I bitch and complain and try to argue, but a few hours later I come sulking back and admit that she was right. And holy crap she makes me a better person, even though I hate hearing it at the time.

When our highest priority is to always make ourselves feel good, or to always make our partner feel good, then nobody ends up feeling good. And our relationship falls apart without our even knowing it.

Without conflict, there can be no trust. Conflict exists

to show us who is there for us unconditionally and who is just there for the benefits. No one trusts a yes-man. If Disappointment Panda were here, he'd tell you that the pain in our relationship is necessary to cement our trust in each other and produce greater intimacy.

For a relationship to be healthy, both people must be willing and able to both say no and hear no. Without that negation, without that occasional rejection, boundaries break down and one person's problems and values come to dominate the other's. Conflict is not only normal, then; it's *absolutely necessary* for the maintenance of a healthy relationship. If two people who are close are not able to hash out their differences openly and vocally, then the relationship is based on manipulation and misrepresentation, and it will slowly become toxic.

Trust is the most important ingredient in any relationship, for the simple reason that without trust, the relationship doesn't actually *mean* anything. A person could tell you that she loves you, wants to be with you, would give up everything for you, but if you don't trust her, you get no benefit from those statements. You don't feel loved until you trust that the love being expressed toward you comes without any special conditions or baggage attached to it.

This is what's so destructive about cheating. It's not about the sex. It's about the trust that has been destroyed as a result of the sex. Without trust, the relationship can no longer function. So it's either rebuild the trust or say your goodbyes.

I often get emails from people who have been cheated

on by their significant other but want to stay with that partner and are wondering how they can trust him or her again. Without trust, they tell me, the relationship has begun to feel like a burden, like a threat that must be monitored and questioned rather than enjoyed.

The problem here is that most people who get caught cheating apologize and give the "It will never happen again" spiel and that's that, as if penises fell into various orifices completely by accident. Many cheatees accept this response at face value, and don't question the values and fucks given by their partner (pun totally intended); they don't ask themselves whether those values and fucks make their partner a good person to stay with. They're so concerned with holding on to their relationship that they fail to recognize that it's become a black hole consuming their self-respect.

If people cheat, it's because something other than the relationship is more important to them. It may be power over others. It may be validation through sex. It may be giving in to their own impulses. Whatever it is, it's clear that the cheater's values are not aligned in a way to support a healthy relationship. And if the cheater doesn't admit this or come to terms with it, if he just gives the old "I don't know what I was thinking; I was stressed out and drunk and she was there" response, then he lacks the serious self-awareness necessary to solve any relationship problems.

What needs to happen is that cheaters have to start peeling away at their self-awareness onion and figure out what fucked-up values caused them to break the trust of the relationship (and whether they actually still value the relationship). They need to be able to say, "You know what: I am selfish. I care about myself more than the relationship; to be honest, I don't really respect the relationship much at all." If cheaters can't express their shitty values, and show that those values have been overridden, then there's no reason to believe that they can be trusted. And if they can't be trusted, then the relationship is not going to get better or change.

The other factor in regaining trust after it's been broken is a practical one: a track record. If someone breaks your trust, words are nice; but you then need to see a consistent track record of improved behavior. Only then can you begin trusting that the cheater's values are now aligned properly and the person really will change.

Unfortunately, building a track record for trust takes time—certainly a lot more time than it takes to break trust. And during that trust-building period, things are likely to be pretty shitty. So both people in the relationship must be conscious of the struggle they're choosing to undertake.

I use the example of cheating in a romantic relationship, but this process applies to a breach in any relationship. When trust is destroyed, it can be rebuilt only if the following two steps happen: 1) the trust-breaker admits the true values that caused the breach and owns up to them, and 2) the trust-breaker builds a solid track record of improved behavior over time. Without the first step, there should be no attempt at reconciliation in the first place.

Trust is like a china plate. If you break it once, with some care and attention you can put it back together again. But if you break it again, it splits into even more pieces and it takes far longer to piece together again. If you break it more and more times, eventually it shatters to the point where it's impossible to restore. There are too many broken pieces, and too much dust.

Freedom Through Commitment

Consumer culture is very good at making us want more, more, more. Underneath all the hype and marketing is the implication that more is always better. I bought into this idea for years. Make more money, visit more countries, have more experiences, be with more women.

But more is not always better. In fact, the opposite is true. We are actually often happier with less. When we're overloaded with opportunities and options, we suffer from what psychologists refer to as the paradox of choice. Basically, the more options we're given, the less satisfied we become with whatever we choose, because we're aware of all the other options we're potentially forfeiting.

So if you have a choice between two places to live and pick one, you'll likely feel confident and comfortable that you made the right choice. You'll be satisfied with your decision.

But if you have a choice among twenty-eight places to live and pick one, the paradox of choice says that you'll likely spend years agonizing, doubting, and second-guessing yourself, wondering if you really made the "right" choice, and if you're truly maximizing your own happiness. And this anxiety, this desire for certainty and perfection and success, will make you unhappy.

So what do we do? Well, if you're like I used to be, you avoid choosing anything at all. You aim to keep your options open as long as possible. You avoid commitment.

But while investing deeply in one person, one place, one job, one activity might deny us the breadth of experience we'd like, pursuing a breadth of experience denies us the opportunity to experience the rewards of depth of experience. There are some experiences that you can have *only* when you've lived in the same place for five years, when you've been with the same person for over a decade, when you've been working on the same skill or craft for half your lifetime. Now that I'm in my thirties, I can finally recognize that commitment, in its own way, offers a wealth of opportunity and experiences that would otherwise never be available to me, no matter where I went or what I did.

When you're pursuing a wide breadth of experience, there are diminishing returns to each new adventure, each new person or thing. When you've never left your home country, the first country you visit inspires a massive perspective shift, because you have such a narrow experience base to draw on. But when you've been to twenty countries, the twenty-first adds little. And when you've been to fifty, the fifty-first adds even less.

The same goes for material possessions, money, hobbies, jobs, friends, and romantic/sexual partners—all the lame superficial values people choose for themselves. The older you get, the more experienced you get, the less significantly each new experience affects you. The first time I drank at a party was exciting. The hundredth time was fun. The five hundredth time felt like a normal weekend. And the thousandth time felt boring and unimportant.

The big story for me personally over the past few years has been my ability to open myself up to commitment. I've chosen to reject all but the very best people and experiences and values in my life. I shut down all my business projects and decided to focus on writing full-time. Since then, my website has become more popular than I'd ever imagined possible. I've committed to one woman for the long haul and, to my surprise, have found this more rewarding than any of the flings, trysts, and one-night stands I had in the past. I've committed to a single geographic location and doubled down on the handful of my significant, genuine, healthy friendships.

And what I've discovered is something entirely counterintuitive: that there is a freedom and liberation in commitment. I've found *increased* opportunity and upside in rejecting alternatives and distractions in favor of what I've chosen to let truly matter to me.

Commitment gives you freedom because you're no longer distracted by the unimportant and frivolous. Commitment gives you freedom because it hones your attention and focus, directing them toward what is most efficient at making you healthy and happy. Commitment makes decision-making easier and removes any fear of missing out; knowing that what you already have is good enough, why would you ever stress about chasing more, more, more again? Commitment allows you to focus intently on a few highly important goals and achieve a greater degree of success than you otherwise would.

In this way, the rejection of alternatives liberates us—rejection of what does not align with our most important values, with our chosen metrics, rejection of the constant pursuit of breadth without depth.

Yes, breadth of experience is likely necessary and desirable when you're young—after all, you have to go out there and discover what seems worth investing yourself in. But depth is where the gold is buried. And you have to stay committed to something and go deep to dig it up. That's true in relationships, in a career, in building a great lifestyle—in everything.

CHAPTER

9

... And Then You Die

S eek the truth for yourself, and I will meet you there."

That was the last thing Josh ever said to me. He said it ironically, attempting to sound deep while simultaneously making fun of people who attempt to sound deep. He was drunk and high. And he was a good friend.

The most transformational moment of my life occurred when I was nineteen years old. My friend Josh had taken me to a party on a lake just north of Dallas, Texas. There were condos on a hill and below the hill was a pool, and below the pool was a cliff overlooking the lake. It was a small cliff, maybe thirty feet high—certainly high enough to give you a second thought about jumping, but low enough that with the right combination of alcohol and peer pressure that second thought could easily vanish.

Shortly after arriving at the party, Josh and I sat in the

pool together, drinking beers and talking as young angsty males do. We talked about drinking and bands and girls and all of the cool stuff Josh had done that summer since dropping out of music school. We talked about playing in a band together and moving to New York City—an impossible dream at the time.

We were just kids.

"Is it okay to jump off that?" I asked after a while, nodding toward the cliff over the lake.

"Yeah," Josh said, "people do it all the time here."

"Are you going to do it?"

He shrugged. "Maybe. We'll see."

Later in the evening, Josh and I got separated. I had become distracted by a pretty Asian girl who liked video games, which to me, as a teenage nerd, was akin to winning the lottery. She had no interest in me, but she was friendly and happy to let me talk, so I talked. After a few beers, I gathered enough courage to ask her to go up to the house with me to get some food. She said sure.

As we walked up the hill, we bumped into Josh coming down. I asked him if he wanted food, but he declined. I asked him where I could find him later on. He smiled and said, "Seek the truth for yourself, and I will meet you there!"

I nodded and made a serious face. "Okay, I'll see you there," I replied, as if everyone knew exactly where the truth was and how to get to it.

Josh laughed and walked down the hill toward the cliff. I laughed and continued up the hill toward the house.

I don't remember how long I was inside. I just remember

that when the girl and I came out again, everyone was gone and there were sirens. The pool was empty. People were running down the hill toward the shoreline below the cliff. There were others already down by the water. I could make out a couple guys swimming around. It was dark and hard to see. The music droned on, but nobody listened.

Still not putting two-and-two together, I hurried down to the shoreline, gnawing on my sandwich, curious as to what everyone was looking at. Halfway down, the pretty Asian girl said to me, "I think something terrible has happened."

When I got to the bottom of the hill, I asked someone where Josh was. No one looked at me or acknowledged me. Everyone stared at the water. I asked again, and a girl started crying uncontrollably.

That's when I put two-and-two together.

It took scuba divers three hours to find Josh's body at the bottom of the lake. The autopsy would later say that his legs had cramped up due to dehydration from the alcohol, as well as to the impact of the jump from the cliff. It was dark out when he went in, the water layered on the night, black on black. No one could see where his screams for help were coming from. Just the splashes. Just the sounds. His parents later told me that he was a terrible swimmer. I'd had no idea.

It took me twelve hours to let myself cry. I was in my car, driving back home to Austin the next morning. I called my dad and told him that I was still near Dallas and that I was going to miss work. (I'd been working for him that summer.) He asked, "Why; what happened? Is everything all right?" And that's when it all came out: the waterworks. The wails and the screams and the snot. I pulled the car over to the side of the road and clutched the phone and cried the way a little boy cries to his father.

I went into a deep depression that summer. I thought I'd been depressed before, but this was a whole new level of meaninglessness—sadness so deep that it physically hurt. People would come by and try to cheer me up, and I would sit there and hear them say all the right things and do all the right things; and I would tell them thank you and how nice it was of them to come over, and I would fake a smile and lie and say that it was getting better, but underneath I just felt nothing.

I dreamed about Josh for a few months after that. Dreams where he and I would have full-blown conversations about life and death, as well as about random, pointless things. Up until that point in my life, I had been a pretty typical middle-class stoner kid: lazy, irresponsible, socially anxious, and deeply insecure. Josh, in many ways, had been a person I looked up to. He was older, more confident, more experienced, and more accepting of and open to the world around him. In one of my last dreams of Josh, I was sitting in a Jacuzzi with him (yeah, I know, weird), and I said something like, "I'm really sorry you died." He laughed. I don't remember exactly what his words were, but he said something like, "Why do you care that I'm dead when you're still so afraid to live?" I woke up crying.

It was sitting on my mom's couch that summer, staring into the so-called abyss, seeing the endless and incomprehensible nothingness where Josh's friendship used to be, when I came to the startling realization that if there really is no reason to do anything, then there is also no reason to *not* do anything; that in the face of the inevitability of death, there is no reason to ever give in to one's fear or embarrassment or shame, since it's all just a bunch of nothing anyway; and that by spending the majority of my short life avoiding what was painful and uncomfortable, I had essentially been avoiding being alive at all.

That summer, I gave up the weed and the cigarettes and the video games. I gave up my silly rock star fantasies and dropped out of music school and signed up for college courses. I started going to the gym and lost a bunch of weight. I made new friends. I got my first girlfriend. For the first time in my life I actually studied for classes, gaining me the startling realization that I could make good grades if only I gave a shit. The next summer, I challenged myself to read fifty nonfiction books in fifty days, and then did it. The following year, I transferred to an excellent university on the other side of the country, where I excelled for the first time, both academically and socially.

Josh's death marks the clearest before/after point I can identify in my life. Pre-tragedy, I was inhibited, unambitious, forever obsessed and confined by what I imagined the world might be thinking of me. Post-tragedy, I morphed into a new person: responsible, curious, hardworking. I still had my insecurities and my baggage—as we always do—but now I gave a fuck about something more important than my insecurities and my baggage.

And that made all the difference. Oddly, it was someone else's death that gave me permission to finally live. And perhaps the worst moment of my life was also the most transformational.

Death scares us. And because it scares us, we avoid thinking about it, talking about it, sometimes even acknowledging it, even when it's happening to someone close to us.

Yet, in a bizarre, backwards way, death is the light by which the shadow of all of life's meaning is measured. Without death, everything would feel inconsequential, all experience arbitrary, all metrics and values suddenly zero.

Something Beyond Our Selves

Ernest Becker was an academic outcast. In 1960, he got his Ph.D. in anthropology; his doctoral research compared the unlikely and unconventional practices of Zen Buddhism and psychoanalysis. At the time, Zen was seen as something for hippies and drug addicts, and Freudian psychoanalysis was considered a quack form of psychology left over from the Stone Age.

In his first job as an assistant professor, Becker quickly fell into a crowd that denounced the practice of psychiatry as a form of fascism. They saw the practice as an unscientific form of oppression against the weak and helpless.

The problem was that Becker's boss was a psychiatrist. So it was kind of like walking into your first job and proudly comparing your boss to Hitler.

As you can imagine, he was fired.

So Becker took his radical ideas somewhere that they

might be accepted: Berkeley, California. But this, too, didn't last long.

Because it wasn't just his anti-establishment tendencies that got Becker into trouble; it was his odd teaching methods as well. He would use Shakespeare to teach psychology, psychology textbooks to teach anthropology, and anthropological data to teach sociology. He'd dress up as King Lear and do mock sword fights in class and go on long political rants that had little to do with the lesson plan. His students adored him. The other faculty loathed him. Less than a year later, he was fired again.

Becker then landed at San Francisco State University, where he actually kept his job for more than a year. But when student protests erupted over the Vietnam War, the university called in the National Guard and things got violent. When Becker sided with the students and publicly condemned the actions of the dean (again, his boss being Hitleresque and everything), he was, once again, promptly fired.

Becker changed jobs four times in six years. And before he could get fired from the fifth, he got colon cancer. The prognosis was grim. He spent the next few years bedridden and had little hope of surviving. So Becker decided to write a book. This book would be about death.

Becker died in 1974. His book *The Denial of Death*, would win the Pulitzer Prize and become one of the most influential intellectual works of the twentieth century, shaking up the fields of psychology and anthropology, while making profound philosophical claims that are still influential today.

The Denial of Death essentially makes two points:

1. Humans are unique in that we're the only animals that can conceptualize and think about ourselves abstractly. Dogs don't sit around and worry about their career. Cats don't think about their past mistakes or wonder what would have happened if they'd done something differently. Monkeys don't argue over future possibilities, just as fish don't sit around wondering if other fish would like them more if they had longer fins.

   As humans, we're blessed with the ability to imagine ourselves in hypothetical situations, to contemplate both the past and the future, to imagine other realities or situations where things might be different. And it's because of this unique mental ability, Becker says, that we all, at some point, become aware of the inevitability of our own death. Because we're able to conceptualize alternate versions of reality, we are also the only animal capable of imagining a reality without ourselves in it.

   This realization causes what Becker calls "death terror," a deep existential anxiety that underlies *everything* we think or do.

2. Becker's second point starts with the premise that we essentially have two "selves." The first self is the physical self—the one that eats, sleeps, snores, and poops. The second self is our conceptual self—our identity, or how we see ourselves.

   Becker's argument is this: We are all aware on some

level that our physical self will eventually die, that this death is inevitable, and that its inevitability—on some unconscious level—scares the shit out of us. Therefore, in order to compensate for our fear of the inevitable loss of our physical self, we try to construct a conceptual self that will live forever. This is why people try so hard to put their names on buildings, on statues, on spines of books. It's why we feel compelled to spend so much time giving ourselves to others, especially to children, in the hopes that our influence—our conceptual self—will last way beyond our physical self. That we will be remembered and revered and idolized long after our physical self ceases to exist.

Becker called such efforts our "immortality projects," projects that allow our conceptual self to live on way past the point of our physical death. All of human civilization, he says, is basically a result of immortality projects: the cities and governments and structures and authorities in place today were all immortality projects of men and women who came before us. They are the remnants of conceptual selves that ceased to die. Names like Jesus, Muhammad, Napoleon, and Shakespeare are just as powerful today as when those men lived, if not more so. And that's the whole point. Whether it be through mastering an art form, conquering a new land, gaining great riches, or simply having a large and loving family that will live on for generations, *all the meaning in our life is shaped by this innate desire to never truly die.*

Religion, politics, sports, art, and technological innovation are the result of people's immortality projects. Becker argues that wars and revolutions and mass murder occur when one group of people's immortality projects rub up against another group's. Centuries of oppression and the bloodshed of millions have been justified as the defense of one group's immortality project against another's.

But, when our immortality projects fail, when the meaning is lost, when the prospect of our conceptual self outliving our physical self no longer seems possible or likely, death terror—that horrible, depressing anxiety—creeps back into our mind. Trauma can cause this, as can shame and social ridicule. As can, as Becker points out, mental illness.

If you haven't figured it out yet, our immortality projects are our values. They are the barometers of meaning and worth in our life. And when our values fail, so do we, psychologically speaking. What Becker is saying, in essence, is that we're all driven by fear to give way too many fucks about something, because giving a fuck about something is the only thing that distracts us from the reality and inevitability of our own death. And to truly not give a single fuck is to achieve a quasi-spiritual state of embracing the impermanence of one's own existence. In that state, one is far less likely to get caught up in various forms of entitlement.

Becker later came to a startling realization on his deathbed: that people's immortality projects were actually the problem, not the solution; that rather than attempting to implement, often through lethal force, their conceptual self across the world, people should question their conceptual self and become more comfortable with the reality of their own death. Becker called this "the bitter antidote," and struggled with reconciling it himself as he stared down his own demise. While death is bad, it is inevitable. Therefore, we should not avoid this realization, but rather come to terms with it as best we can. Because once we become comfortable with the fact of our own death—the root terror, the underlying anxiety motivating all of life's frivolous ambitions—we can then choose our values more freely, unrestrained by the illogical quest for immortality, and freed from dangerous dogmatic views.

The Sunny Side of Death

I step from rock to rock, climbing steadily, leg muscles stretching and aching. In that trancelike state that comes from slow, repetitive physical exertion, I'm nearing the top. The sky gets wide and deep. I'm alone now. My friends are far below me, taking pictures of the ocean.

Finally, I climb over a small boulder and the view opens up. I can see from here to the infinite horizon. It feels as though I'm staring at the edge of the earth, where water meets the sky, blue on blue. The wind screams across my skin. I look up. It's bright. It's beautiful.

I'm at South Africa's Cape of Good Hope, once thought to be the southern tip of Africa and the southernmost point in the world. It's a tumultuous place, a place full of storms and treacherous waters. A place that's seen centuries of trade and commerce and human endeavor. A place, ironically, of lost hopes.

There is a saying in Portuguese: *Ele dobra o Cabo Boa Esperança.* It means, "He's rounding the Cape of Good Hope." Ironically, it means that the person's life is in its final phase, that he's incapable of accomplishing anything more.

I step across the rocks toward the blue, allowing its vastness to engulf my field of vision. I'm sweating yet cold. Excited yet nervous. *Is this it?*

The wind is slapping my ears. I hear nothing, but I see the edge: where the rock meets oblivion. I stop and stand for a moment, several yards away. I can see the ocean below, lapping and frothing against cliffs stretching out for miles to either side. The tides are furious against the impenetrable walls. Straight ahead, it's a sheer drop of at least fifty yards to the water below.

To my right, tourists are dotted across the landscape below, snapping photos and aggregating themselves into antlike formations. To my left is Asia. In front of me is the sky and behind me is everything I've ever hoped for and brought with me.

What if this is it? What if this is all there is?

I look around. I'm alone. I take my first step toward the edge of the cliff.

The human body seems to come equipped with a natural radar for death-inducing situations. For example, the moment you get within about ten feet of a cliff edge, minus guardrail, a certain tension digs into your body. Your back stiffens. Your skin ripples. Your eyes become hyperfocused on every detail of your environment. Your feet feel as though they're made of rock. It's as if there were a big, invisible magnet gently pulling your body back to safety.

But I fight the magnet. I drag the feet made of rock closer to the edge.

At five feet away, your mind joins the party. You can now see not only the edge of the cliff, but *down* the cliff face itself, which induces all sorts of unwanted visualizations of tripping and falling and tumbling to a splashy death. It's really fucking far, your mind reminds you. Like, *really* fucking far. *Dude, what are you doing? Stop moving. Stop it.*

I tell my mind to shut up, and keep inching forward.

At three feet, your body goes into full-scale red alert. You are now within an errant shoelace-trip of your life ending. It feels as though a hefty gust of wind could send you sailing off into that blue-bisected eternity. Your legs shake. As do your hands. As does your voice, in case you need to remind yourself you're not about to plummet to your death.

The three-foot distance is most people's absolute limit. It's just close enough to lean forward and catch a glimpse of the bottom, but still far enough to feel as though you're not at any real risk of killing yourself. Standing that close to the edge of a cliff, even one as beautiful and mesmerizing as the Cape of Good Hope, induces a heady sense of vertigo, and threatens to regurgitate any recent meal.

Is this it? Is this all there is? Do I already know everything I will ever know?

I take another microstep, then another. Two feet now. My forward leg vibrates as I put the weight of my body on it. I shuffle on. Against the magnet. Against my mind. Against all my better instincts for survival.

One foot now. I'm now looking straight down the cliff face. I feel a sudden urge to cry. My body instinctively crouches, protecting itself against something imagined and inexplicable. The wind comes in hailstorms. The thoughts come in right hooks.

At one foot you feel like you're floating. Anything but looking straight down feels as though you're part of the sky itself. You actually kind of expect to fall at this point.

I crouch there for a moment, catching my breath, collecting my thoughts. I force myself to stare down at the water hitting the rocks below me. Then I look again to my right, at the little ants milling about the signage below me, snapping photos, chasing tour buses, on the off chance that somebody somehow sees me. This desire for attention is wholly irrational. But so is all of this. It's impossible to make me out up here, of course. And even if it weren't, there's nothing that those distant people could say or do.

All I hear is the wind.

Is this it?

My body shudders, the fear becoming euphoric and blinding. I focus my mind and clear my thoughts in a kind of meditation. Nothing makes you present and mindful like being mere inches away from your own death. I straighten up and look out again, and find myself smiling. I remind myself that it's all right to die.

This willing and even exuberant interfacing with one's own mortality has ancient roots. The Stoics of ancient Greece and Rome implored people to keep death in mind at all times, in order to appreciate life more and remain humble in the face of its adversities. In various forms of Buddhism, the practice of meditation is often taught as a means of preparing oneself for death while still remaining alive. Dissolving one's ego into an expansive nothingness—achieving the enlightened state of nirvana—is seen as a trial run of letting oneself cross to the other side. Even Mark Twain, that hairy goofball who came in and left on Halley's Comet, said, "The fear of death follows from the fear of life. A man who lives fully is prepared to die at any time."

Back on the cliff, I bend down, slightly leaning back. I put my hands on the ground behind me and gently lower myself onto my butt. I then gradually slide one leg over the edge of the cliff. There's a small rock jutting out of the cliff side. I rest my foot on it. Then I slide my other foot off the edge and put it on the same small rock. I sit there a moment, leaning back on my palms, wind ruffling my hair. The anxiety is bearable now, as long as I stay focused on the horizon.

Then I sit up straight and look down the cliff again. Fear shoots back up through my spine, electrifying my limbs and laser-focusing my mind on the exact coordinates of every inch of my body. The fear is stifling at times. But each time it stifles me, I empty my thoughts, focus my attention on the bottom of the cliff below me, force myself to gaze at my potential doom, and then to simply acknowledge its existence.

I was now sitting on the edge of the world, at the southern-most tip of hope, the gateway to the east. The feeling was exhilarating. I can feel the adrenaline pumping through my body. Being so still, so conscious, never felt so thrilling. I listen to the wind and watch the ocean and look out upon the ends of the earth—and then I laugh with the light, all that it touches being good.

Confronting the reality of our own mortality is important because it obliterates all the crappy, fragile, superficial values in life. While most people whittle their days chasing another buck, or a little bit more fame and attention, or a little bit more assurance that they're right or loved, death confronts all of us with a far more painful and important question: What is your legacy?

How will the world be different and better when you're gone? What mark will you have made? What influence will you have caused? They say that a butterfly flapping its wings in Africa can cause a hurricane in Florida; well, what hurricanes will you leave in your wake?

As Becker pointed out, this is arguably the *only* truly important question in our life. Yet we avoid thinking about it. One, because it's hard. Two, because it's scary. Three, because we have no fucking clue what we're doing.

And when we avoid this question, we let trivial and hateful values hijack our brains and take control of our desires and ambitions. Without acknowledging the ever-present gaze of death, the superficial will appear important, and the important will appear superficial. Death is the only thing we can know with any certainty. And as such, it must be the compass by which we orient all of our other values and decisions. It is the correct answer to all of the questions we should ask but never do. The only way to be comfortable with death is to understand and see yourself as something bigger than yourself; to choose values that stretch beyond serving yourself, that are simple and immediate and controllable and tolerant of the chaotic world around you. This is the basic root of all happiness. Whether you're listening to Aristotle or the psychologists at Harvard or Jesus Christ or the goddamn Beatles, they all say that happiness comes from the same thing: caring about something greater than yourself, believing that you are a contributing component in some much larger entity, that your life is but a mere side process of some great unintelligible production. This feeling is what people go to church for; it's what they fight in wars for; it's what they raise families and save pensions and build bridges and invent cell phones for: this fleeting sense of being part of something greater and more unknowable than themselves.

And entitlement strips this away from us. The gravity of entitlement sucks all attention inward, toward ourselves, causing us to feel as though *we* are at the center of all of the problems in the universe, that *we* are the one suffering all of the injustices, that *we* are the one who deserves greatness over all others.

As alluring as it is, entitlement isolates us. Our curiosity and excitement for the world turns in upon itself and reflects our own biases and projections onto every person we meet and every event we experience. This feels sexy and enticing and may feel good for a while and sells a lot of tickets, but it's spiritual poison.

It's these dynamics that plague us now. We are so materially well off, yet so psychologically tormented in so many low-level and shallow ways. People relinquish all responsibility, demanding that society cater to *their* feelings and sensibilities. People hold on to arbitrary certainties and try to enforce them on others, often violently, in the name of some made-up righteous cause. People, high on a sense of false superiority, fall into inaction and lethargy for fear of trying something worthwhile and failing at it.

The pampering of the modern mind has resulted in a population that feels deserving of something without earning that something, a population that feels they have a right to something without sacrificing for it. People declare themselves experts, entrepreneurs, inventors, innovators, mavericks, and coaches without any real-life experience. And they do this not because they actually think they *are* greater than everybody else; they do it because they feel that they *need to be great* to be accepted in a world that broadcasts only the extraordinary.

Our culture today confuses great attention and great success, assuming them to be the same thing. But they are not.

You *are* great. Already. Whether you realize it or not. Whether anybody else realizes it or not. And it's not because you launched an iPhone app, or finished school a year early, or bought yourself a sweet-ass boat. These things do not define greatness.

You are already great because in the face of endless confusion and certain death, you continue to choose what to give a fuck about and what not to. This mere fact, this simple optioning for your own values in life, already makes you beautiful, already makes you successful, and already makes you loved. Even if you don't realize it. Even if you're sleeping in a gutter and starving.

You too are going to die, and that's because you too were fortunate enough to have lived. You may not feel this. But go stand on a cliff sometime, and maybe you will.

Bukowski once wrote, "We're all going to die, all of us. What a circus! That alone should make us love each other, but it doesn't. We are terrorized and flattened by life's trivialities; we are eaten up by nothing."

Looking back on that night, out by that lake, when I watched my friend Josh's body getting fished out of the lake by paramedics. I remember staring into the black Texas night and watching my ego slowly dissolve into it. Josh's death taught me much more than I initially realized. Yes, it helped me to seize the day, to take responsibility for my choices, and to pursue my dreams with less shame and inhibition.

But these were side effects of a deeper, more primary lesson. And the primary lesson was this: there is nothing to be afraid of. Ever. And reminding myself of my own death repeatedly over the years—whether it be through meditation, through reading philosophy, or through doing crazy shit like standing on a cliff in South Africa—is the only thing that has helped me hold this realization front and center in my mind. This acceptance of my death, this understanding of my own fragility, has made everything easier—untangling my addictions, identifying and confronting my own entitlement, accepting responsibility for my own problems—suffering through my fears and uncertainties, accepting my failures and embracing rejections—it has all been made lighter by the thought of my own death. The more I peer into the darkness, the brighter life gets, the quieter the world becomes, and the less unconscious resistance I feel to, well, anything.

I sit there on the Cape for a few minutes, taking in everything. When I finally decide to get up, I put my hands behind me and scoot back. Then, slowly, I stand. I check the ground around me—making sure there's no errant rock ready to sabotage me. Having recognized that I am safe, I begin to walk back to reality—five feet, ten feet—my body restoring itself with each step. My feet become lighter. I let life's magnet draw me in.

As I step back over some rocks, back to the main path, I look up to see a man staring at me. I stop and make eye contact with him.

"Um. I saw you sitting on the edge over there," he says. His accent is Australian. The word "there" rolls out of his mouth awkwardly. He points toward Antarctica.

"Yeah. The view is gorgeous, isn't it?" I am smiling. He is not. He has a serious look on his face.

I brush my hands off on my shorts, my body still buzzing from my surrender. There's an awkward silence.

The Aussie stands for a moment, perplexed, still looking at me, clearly thinking of what to say next. After a moment, he carefully pieces the words together.

"Is everything okay? How are you feeling?"

I pause for a moment, still smiling. "Alive. Very alive."

His skepticism breaks and reveals a smile in its place. He gives a slight nod and heads down the trail. I stand above, taking in the view, waiting for my friends to arrive on the peak.

ACKNOWLEDGMENTS

This book began as a big, messy thing and required more than just my own hands to chisel something comprehensible out of it.

First and foremost, thank you to my brilliant and beautiful wife, Fernanda, who never hesitates to say no to me when I need to hear it most. Not only do you make me a better person, but your unconditional love and constant feedback during the writing process were indispensable.

To my parents, for putting up with my shit all these years and continuing to love me anyway. In many ways, I don't feel as though I fully became an adult until I understood many of the concepts in this book. In that sense, it's been a joy to get to know you as an adult these past few years. And to my brother as well: I never doubt the existence of mutual love and respect between us, even if I sometimes get butt-hurt that you don't text me back.

To Philip Kemper and Drew Birnie—two big brains that conspire to make my brain appear much larger than it actually is. Your hard work and brilliance continue to floor me.

To Michael Covell, for being my intellectual stress test, especially when it comes to understanding psychological research, and for always challenging me on my assumptions. To my editor, Luke Dempsey, for mercilessly tightening the screws on my writing, and for possibly having an even fouler mouth than I do. To my agent, Mollie Glick, for helping me define the vision for the book and pushing it much farther into the world than I ever expected to see it go. To Taylor Pearson, Dan Andrews, and Jodi Ettenberg, for their support during this process; you three kept me both accountable and sane, which are the only two things every writer needs.

And finally, to the millions of people who, for whatever reason, decided to read a potty-mouthed asshole from Boston writing about life on his blog. The flood of emails I've received from those of you willing to open up the most intimate corners of your life to me, a complete stranger, both humbles me and inspires me. At this point in my life, I've spent thousands of hours reading and studying these subjects. But you all continue to be my true education. Thank you.